Y0-BVO-654

URBAN
HOMESTEADING

URBAN HOMESTEADING

Programs and Policies

MITTIE OLION CHANDLER

Studies in Social Welfare Policies and Programs,
Number 9

GREENWOOD PRESS
New York • Westport, Connecticut • London

Library of Congress Cataloging-in-Publication Data

Chandler, Mittie Olion.
    Urban homesteading : programs and policies / Mittie Olion
Chandler.
        p.   cm. — (Studies in social welfare policies and programs,
    ISSN 8755-5360 ; no. 9)
    Bibliography: p.
    Includes index.
    ISBN 0-313-26338-8 (lib. bdg. : alk. paper)
    1. Urban homesteading—United States—Case studies.   2. Urban
homesteading—Maryland—Baltimore.   3. Urban homesteading—Michigan—
Detroit.   4. Urban homesteading—Pennsylvania—Philadelphia.
I. Title.   II. Series.
HD7289.42.U6C47 1988
363.5'8—dc19   88-15481

British Library Cataloguing in Publication Data is available.

Library of Congress Catalog Card Number: 88-15481
ISBN: 0-313-26338-8
ISSN: 8755-5360

First published in 1988

Greenwood Press, Inc.
88 Post Road West, Westport, Connecticut 06881

Printed in the United States of America

The paper used in this book complies with the
Permanent Paper Standard issued by the National
Information Standards Organization (Z39.48-1984).

10 9 8 7 6 5 4 3 2 1

Contents

Tables and Figure

Acknowledgments

The personal and professional support I have received has culminated in the completion of this project. What began as an inquiry about the efficiency of the Detroit urban homesteading program in 1981 evolved into a project to initially research three cities' programs. The scope of this investigation is still expanding.

I would like to recognize the assistance of the research support provided by the College of Urban Affairs at Cleveland State University. The encouragement of Dr. Susan MacManus, a former colleague, was instrumental to the pursuit of this project.

The unselfish sacrifices of my husband, Everett, and my daughter, Mae Evette, during the final phases of transforming this manuscript into publishable form have been appreciated. This book is dedicated to my mother, Lurie Mae Davis, and my grandmother, Mittie Taylor.

1

Introduction

The subject of this book is the implementation of the Section 810 Urban Homesteading Program in three cities: Baltimore, Detroit, and Philadelphia. Enacted under the Housing and Community Development Act of 1974, Section 810 provides for the transfer of federally owned, unoccupied one- to four-family residences to states or units of general local government or their designated public agencies for use in approved urban homesteading programs. Participating localities or agencies then transfer the properties to prospective homeowners--without substantial cost--for rehabilitation and occupancy. Urban homesteading can achieve a number of related objectives: it can conserve decaying housing resources; It can stabilize and revitalize neighborhoods by removing blighting influences; it can make available standard housing and homeownership for households of modest means.

In administering the program, the Department of Housing and Urban Development (HUD) purportedly aims to provide broad administrative guidelines rather than strict regulations that might limit program flexibility. Decisions regarding program design and administration are left to the localities. Participating localities are also allowed to establish the specific goals that urban homesteading is to address at the local level. Section 810's emphasis on local control is unique in a narrow-purpose categorical program for housing. By definition, a categorical grant is earmarked for a specific governmental purpose by the grantor. Stipulations usually set forth in these grants are intended to restrain rather than to empower recipients.

The main issue is the significance of local discretion in implementing Section 810: Is significant discretion extended in substantive areas? Does the degree of flexibility given to localities affect the attainment of national objectives? How do local conditions influence program outcomes? Does localization of public policy improve the quality of decision making?

RESEARCH DIRECTIONS

     The urban homesteading concept is historically rooted in
the homesteading efforts of the 1860s that contributed to
the settlement of the western United States.   As a proposed
means of reclaiming declining neighborhoods, urban
homesteading enjoyed fleeting popularity in the early 1970s.
For a brief period, the media embraced the notion of urban
pioneers salvaging communities.   Enthusiasm waned as the
reality of operating the program tempered the idealism of
the implementing agencies and prospective beneficiaries.
Section 810 Urban Homesteading did not have a major impact
in any city studied.   However, outcomes did vary
considerably.   This research determined that the factors
accounting for this observed variation were inherent in the
legislation and the unique local circumstances of the
participating cities.
     Urban homesteading was not a federal invention.   Several
programs were initiated by local governments in 1973 using
locally owned properties.   The federal government did not
become officially involved until 1974, with the passage of
Section 810 legislation.   Under Section 810, the federal
government provides properties--but no funds for their
rehabilitation or program administration.   Participating
localities are required to obtain that support from other
sources.   Paradoxically, the Housing and Community
Development Act of 1974 was the enabling legislation for
both Section 810 and the Community Development Block Grant
(CDBG) Program.   The no strings character of block grants
for broad governmental purposes contrasts with the
requirements attached to categorical grants.   CDBG is the
primary source of community development funds for housing
and community development activities in urban areas.
Reservations under the Section 312 Rehabilitation Loan
Program--another federal program--are available for
financing rehabilitation of single-family and multi-family
homesteading properties as well as other properties within
the urban homesteading neighborhoods.   Section 312 funds
have been provided for rehabilitation since 1964 and
continue to be a major source.   In effect, localities which
chose to participate in Section 810 Urban Homesteading were
required to divert some of their CDBG and Section 312
allocations to that program.   Urban homesteading did not
fare well in cities where it was in tight competition for
rehabilitation and administrative dollars.   Local conditions
and priorities affected these decisions and, in turn,
program outcomes.
     Since Section 810 Urban Homesteading is a relatively
small effort compared to other housing and community
development programs, it permits an in-depth look at program
adaptation related to local implementation of public policy.
Within the parameters of the federal administrative
guidelines, participating localities had considerable
decision-making authority.   As expected, there was variation
in areas specified in the legislation, such as selection of
homesteaders and homestead properties.   The impact upon

program output, however, was minimal. The political and practical reasons behind local responses to program guidelines are set forth in this book. Localities differed in their adherence to program conditions that affected program outcomes. Political backing for the program seemed to influence the likelihood of local officials to deviate.

Goal setting, as was mentioned, was delegated to localities participating in urban homesteading. The establishment of program goals is a pivotal issue. Allowing for unique local conditions is a key concern in the design the programs that are national in scope. The discretion afforded in urban homesteading gave local policymakers the responsibility for integrating the program into their unique environments. Implicitly, the goals established became benchmarks for evaluating program accomplishments. In reality, the exercise of discretion was limited by the seemingly innocuous guidelines.

RESEARCH DESIGN

This study examines urban homesteading from its beginning as a local initiative in 1973 through its federal enactment in 1974 and to its operation until May 1986. Baltimore, Detroit, and Philadelphia. Case studies of the three cities, by definition, lend themselves to describing the idiosyncrasies of each instance. Program results are influenced by differences in demographic characteristics, political cultures, and community development approaches among cities.

Each city developed urban homesteading concepts on two levels--federal and local. While the federal program is the primary focus of this research, the details of the local programs are included for comparative purposes. The federal program (implemented by localities) is referred to interchangeably as Section 810 Urban Homesteading, Section 810, or urban homesteading. The locally enacted programs are referred to in the vernacular of the particular program. When referenced conceptually, the generic term "urban homesteading" is used.

The Section 810 legislation remained virtually unchanged from 1974 to 1984. Unless otherwise indicated, references to the legislation, rules, and regulations apply primarily to the original provisions. The circumstances and details of the revisions in 1984 are discussed later. They are a part of the Housing and Urban-Rural Recovery Act of 1983.

Data for this study were gathered from primary and secondary sources. Officials in each city completed a questionnaire that provided a common information base. Personal interviews took place with at least one official in each city who was responsible for operating Section 810 and local urban homesteading programs as well as with HUD area office officials assigned to each Section 810 program. Additional interviews were held with persons currently and previously associated with the Section 810 Program at HUD headquarters in Washington, D.C. These discussions provided not only valuable data but additional insight about interactions among officials at different levels.

This study draws on a number of government reports and documents related to the federal and local urban homesteading programs. Documents on related topics, such as CDBGs were also utilized. These reports provided a historical and legislative perspective on the development of urban homesteading. Scholarly works, particularly related to the first urban homesteading efforts, were useful to this project.

The following issues were explored:

1. Attitudes and experiences of local government, the HUD area office, and central office personnel with respect to one another and the operation of Section 810 Urban Homesteading.

2. Prevailing influences on the respective city's implementation plan, i.e., elected officials, community groups, and others.

3. Effects of federal grants on local autonomy and decision making.

4. Ambiguity between organizational goals and policy implementation.

5. Methods of urban homesteading program implementation in each city within the scope of local government.

6. Program adaptation in different political environments and in different organizational settings.

7. Significance of basic policy decisions that determine outcomes (neighborhood designation, property selection, homesteader selection, financing arrangements, management of rehabilitation) and how they reflected political or program objectives.

8. Consequences of the program, e.g., income groups served, incidence of gentrification and/or displacement.

9. The community development history of each city in order to discern the role of urban homesteading as a community development.

10. Housing and community development performance records of the cities with particular emphasis on urban homesteading.

CHAPTER ORGANIZATION

As a federal categorical program, urban homesteading was illuminated through a rich literature on federalism, intergovernmental relations, and policy implementation. This theoretical foundation is addressed in Chapter 2. A chronology of housing and community development efforts is reviewed to garner a historical foundation for the study of urban homesteading. The basic themes and constructs are presented in Chapter 3.

The subject cities for this study were chosen on the bases of both their similarities and their differences. Baltimore, Detroit, and Philadelphia are urban areas that share certain demographic and socioeconomic features. From the standpoint of federal intervention and relationships, the three have been subject to similar legislation and directives as central cities in metropolitan areas. In Chapter 4, the cities are described and observations are made in how local fiscal, political, and community development issues are managed.

In Chapter 5, variations in urban homesteading implementation, the legislative history of Section 810 Urban Homesteading, and a description of Section 810 implementation in each city are discussed. Local versions of urban homesteading are described and compared with the federal program.

The research findings from all three cities constitute Chapters 6 and 7. In Chapter 6, urban homesteading operations among the cities are assessed and compared. In Chapter 7, specific sources of program variation are presented and generalized as applicable to other programs. The conclusions and findings are summarized and their theoretical implications are assessed in Chapter 8.

2

Urban Homesteading Within the Context of Federalism and Implementation

Section 810 Urban Homesteading is a hybrid: a narrow-purpose categorical program with features of decentralization. The elements of decentralization are the discretion and flexibility given to the participating localities and to HUD area offices in carrying out their roles.

EVOLUTION FROM CATEGORICAL TO BLOCK GRANTS

On a continuum, maximum federal control is generally associated with categorical grants while maximum recipient discretion is usually associated with general revenue sharing. Categorical grants intended for specific, narrowly defined purposes include four types. Formula grants are funds allocated according to factors enumerated in the authorizing legislation. Project grants are awarded by federal administrators to selected applicants on the basis of statutory guidelines. Formula project grants combine project applications and discretionary awards with a statutory formula. Open-end reimbursements are provided by the federal government to state and local governments for a fixed proportion of their program costs. In general, project grants place more restraints on recipients because federal administrators can require precise performance conditions and narrowly circumscribe the scope of permitted activities.

Block grants fall between categorical grants and general revenue sharing. Block grants are commonly defined as programs "in which funds are provided chiefly to general purpose governmental units in accordance with a statutory formula for use in a broad functional area largely at the recipient's discretion."[1] Implementation at the local level is relatively unrestricted within the programmatic guidelines.

The enactment of Section 810 Urban Homesteading and Community Development Block Grants within the same legislative package (Housing and Community Development Act of 1974) reflect the disparate views within Congress about

local control.   Kenneth Palmer has found that a particular
type of federal grant can reveal information about the
orientation of a political administration toward the issue
of centralization of control.[2]

Project grants experienced their heyday between 1965 and
1969.   Providing discretion to federal administrators and
greater leverage than formula grants, project grants
flourished as federal aid programs set forth national objectives and enlisted subnational governments in carrying out
such goals.[3]

As federal control increased, concern mounted about the
recipient governments' degree of flexibility in using
federal aid.   This, in part,   led to the establishment of
block grants--beginning with the passage of the Partnership
for Health Act of 1966. This act provoked relatively little
controversy, but subsequent legislative efforts did raise
the issue of the desirability of categorical versus block
grants.

Revenue sharing, the centerpiece of the New Federalism
of the Republican years 1969-77, was complemented by the
passage of two block grants.   The Housing and Community
Development Act of 1974 and the Comprehensive Employment and
Training Act (CETA) of 1973 increased the discretion of
state and local officials; over 38,000 subnational general-
purpose governments became part of the federal-aid system
for the first time.   The Housing and Community Development
Act was the largest block grant enacted during the Nixon-
Ford administration, with some $8.45 billion authorized for
the program's first three years.   From 1964 to 1966, 160
project grants (but only 39 formula grants) were added.   The
popularity of project grants generally waned when Congress
enacted general revenue sharing and several new block
grants.

DEPENDENCE ON FEDERAL FUNDS

Federal funds have become a major source of revenue for
Baltimore, Detroit, and Philadelphia.   This dependence is
reflected in their history of federal grants-in-aid
allocations.   (See Table 2.1.) In general, the allocation
of federal dollars to aid state and local governments has
increased steadily since 1932.   While the number of grants
expanded slowly during the 1920s, the amount of aid
available between 1913 and 1932 grew from $12 million to
$232 million, when a precedent was set for a widespread
federal grants-in-aid system.   Not only did the states
receive increased revenue, but cities dealing with the
consequences of the Depression became direct beneficiaries
of federal grants.

Federal aid to states and localities increased from less
than $1 billion in 1940 to $8.5 billion in 1963.
Remarkably, as noted by the Advisory Commission on
Intergovernmental Relations, "the increases over the period
1942-58 merely kept pace with the growth of the economy,
with federal payments to state and local governments holding

Category	Baltimore	Detroit	Philadelphia
TABLE 2.1 FISCAL DATA			
Total Revenue (x 1,000)			
1984	$1,341.9	$1,264.9	$1,943.3
1982-83	1,392.2	1,351.5	1,846.7
1980	1,351.3	1,403.8	2,038.1
1970	636.4	500.7	705.1
1960	221.3	224.3	255.3
% Intergovernmental Sources			
1984	52	46	25
1982-83	58	51	31
1980	62	54	24
1970	53	35	32
1960	37	30	11
Total Expenditures (x 1,000)			
1984	1,194.5	1,106.1	1,838.8
1982-83	1,261.7	1,282.8	1,821.5
1980	1,172.6	1,338.5	2,168.0
1970	668.0	428.6	694.7
1960	215.0	217.4	278.5

Sources: International City Management Association Municipal Year Books, 1962, p. 252; 1973, p. 100; 1983, pp. 26-40; 1987, pp. 192-206, and U.S. Department of Commerce, Bureau of the Census, City Government Finances, 1982-83, pp. 32-50.

roughly constant at about 1 percent of the Gross National Product."[4] The increases in federal intergovernmental grants-in-aid did not deviate from overall economic trends.

With the grants explosion of the Johnson administration, federal aid increased tenfold to more than $80 billion between 1963 and 1978. Federal aid to states and localities represented 7.6 percent of the federal budget in 1960; it topped 17 percent in fiscal 1977. In spite of the efforts to arrest the growth in federal aid, grant obligations doubled during this period. In 1978 almost $77.9 billion was provided to state and local governments. The trend continued during the Carter administration. Grants-in-aid jumped from $58 billion in 1976 to nearly $83 billion in 1979, while the total number of grants reached 492. In 1979, there was actually a decline of 5 percent in the rate of grant-in-aid allocations when adjusted for inflation.

OBJECTIVES OF FEDERAL GRANTS

Each administration since 1965 has had an impact upon
the federal grant system.   The chief concerns of each
administration--and the modifications it tried to bring
about--are revealed   in the   greatly expanded use of
categorical grants to address social problems under Johnson;
the pursuit of devolution under the new federalism of Nixon
and Ford;   and the Carter administration's efforts to
redesign federal grants to target needy localities.[5] The
Reagan era has been marked by attempts to transfer massive
responsibilities to state and   local governments under
another iteration of New Federalism.

The Great Society years were distinguished by a growing
use of grants to pursue distinctively national goals.   At
the same time, the amount of federal influence in local
affairs grew.   New Federalism (under Nixon and Ford) sought
to counter criticism of federal intervention by suggesting
that all levels of government need not be heavily involved
in all policy areas; its fundamental premise was the need to
sort out the appropriate activities at each level.   New
Federalism maintained that the federal government should be
involved in financing most programs,   even when state and
local   governments   controlled   policymaking   and
administration.[6] During the Nixon-Ford period, agencies put
authority in regional field offices and permitted
subnational governments wide latitude.   The   Carter
administration concentrated programs more intensively on
localities distressed by unemployment and poverty.   The
Reagan administration suggested returning some programs to
states and localities as a   way to slow the federal
government's growth.   The possible financial disadvantages
of this scheme have concerned state and local officials and
efforts to carry it out have been unsuccessful thus far.

Though it has historically generated public and media
fanfare, urban homesteading has commanded little legislative
attention.   It has operated innocuously since its enactment,
and has not been directly subjected to the whims of changing
administrations.   Its linkage to CDBG and Section 312 is
another major legislative distinction. As will be discussed
later, the programs are linked legislatively, financially,
and programmatically.   Their   association,   as federal
programs go, may not be especially unusual;   but the
strength of the dependency may be.

IMPLEMENTATION

Implementation has emerged as the primary public policy
problem in the aftermath of the criticism of Great Society
programs.   At the heart of the criticism is the failure of
programs to yield the expected results.   Housing programs
have not been spared such criticism.

The insights of existing literature are relevant to this
study.   Among the concepts   discussed by scholars of
implementation analysis are macro- and micro-implementation
(Berman);   shortcomings of the federal system and lack of

incentives as causes of implementation failure (Derthick); the complexity of joint action as a cause of delay which inhibits implementation success (Pressman and Wildavsky); gamesmanship and the role of a policy entrepreneur or "fixer" in implementation success (Bardach); the strength of statutory variables and tractability of the problem (Sabatier and Mazmanian); achieving national goals within a federal system (Sundquist); adapting federal programs to local conditions (Thomas); and the strength of nonstatutory variables in affecting the achievement of statutory objectives (Marshall, Browning, and Tabb). Pressman and Wildavsky view implementation as an independent variable that explains why programs are or are not carried out as intended as well as a dependent variable that might differ according to the state of society, the condition of the economy, and the changing character of political cleavages. Emphasis is on how forces that produce policy affect implementation, rather than on how implementation affects programs. The perspectives of these researchers illuminate the range of factors that influence implementation.

The contribution of Berman is especially applicable to the processes of urban homesteading implementation. In this depiction, the implementation of national policy involves two classes of problems: macro-implementation --the execution of policy by the federal government to influence local delivery systems in desired ways and micro-implementation --the response of local organizations to federal actions that require the devising and carrying out their own internal policies.

The following factors influence urban homesteading implementation:

1. The discretion afforded to local program implementors in setting goals;
2. The scope of incentives offered to participating localities;
3. Mandates that deter user participation;
4. Political support for local objectives;
5. Characteristics of the implementing agency; and
6. Financial resources for operation.

The discretion and incentives given to localities are shaped by features of macro-implementation: (1) the characteristics of the policy legislation--the extent of multiple, competing, and vague goals with ambiguous directives and (2) the validity of the theory behind the legislation, which will influence the ability to obtain program objectives. Legislation is vague or requires administrative interpretation in some cases because Congress simply fails to understand the complexities of program implementation. In fact, Congress often passes legislation without a clear understanding of the practical consequences or actual costs for state and local governments.[7]

The effects of federal mandates, local political support, implementing agency characteristics, and financial support upon local components are influenced by features of micro-implementation: (1) the influence of the federal government upon local policy--adaptive processes between the policy and local behavior; (2) consonance between national goals and local goals; and (3) variable program effects as determined by local political, social, and economic conditions.

Local Discretion in Goal Setting

The stated purpose of the Section 810 Program is to utilize existing housing stock to provide homeownership, thereby encouraging public and private investment in selected neighborhoods and assisting in neighborhood preservation and revitalization.

Section 810 legislation intentionally avoided setting specific program goals. This is important for two reasons. Goals define, implicitly or explicitly, who the program beneficiaries will be. Goals also are the benchmark against which program outcomes are compared. Given the historical connection of urban homesteading and the CDBG, it is likely that the avoidance of explicit goal setting reflects the political environment in 1974 when both were enacted. During that time, the preference for programmatic decentralization encouraged a local role in goal formulation. Program goals, when presented, are susceptible to ambiguous interpretation by policymakers. When they are not included, as in this legislation, there is even more room for slack.

In this discussion, discretion is associated with loose, if not weak, statutes. For example, localities participating in Section 810 homesteading were to give special consideration to the homesteader's "need for housing" and "capacity to make or cause to be made necessary repairs and improvements." As the result of divergent interpretations of these phrases, persons with incomes ranging from low- to upper-middle participated in Urban Homesteading Programs. Pressman and Wildavsky comment that the more general an idea--and the more adaptable it is to a range of circumstances--the more likely it is to be realized in some form, but the less likely it is to emerge as intended in practice. The more restricted the idea, the more likely it is to emerge as predicted: but the less likely it is to have a significant impact.[8] This view of program detail differs from the position of Sabatier and Mazmanian.

The discretion allowed in urban homesteading may be its Achille's heel, based upon the importance of statutes as discussed by Sabatier and Mazmanian. They find that statutes can structure the implementation process to the extent that they (1) stipulate a set of clear and consistent objectives; (2) incorporate a sound theory relating behavioral change to the objectives; and (3) plan implementation in a manner conducive to attaining the changes. The behavior of various administering agencies under a statute can vary to the extent that it is unstructured. Variables affected by the statute are validity of the underlying causal theory, precise and clear ranking of statutory objectives, financial resources available to the implementing agency, and assignment to implementing agencies committed to statutory objectives. Although Sabatier and Mazmanian focus on regulatory policy, several points are salient to the implementation of the urban homesteading program policy. Key variables that are not provided by the urban homesteading statute--but that affect implementation--are the prioritization of objectives and financial resources for implementation.

If the federal government does not provide goals that focus upon a particular socioeconomic group, the disparity at the local level will probably be greater than observed by Browning, Marshall, and Tabb. They found that grants with strong statutes directed toward benefiting minorities, like Model Cities, result in more local targeting of benefits to minorities than grants with less federal control in that direction, such as CDBG and general revenue sharing. The Section 810 legislation did not specify targeting of any income group until 1984.

Allowing local governments to set urban homesteading goals may permit the federal government to avoid harsh criticism for program shortcomings. A major source of federal program failure has been identified as the centralized orientation inherent in the American federal system. The demise of another ambitious urban development program was attributed to this characteristic. "The failure of New Towns In-Town resulted from the limited ability of the federal government to influence the actions of local governments and from its tendency to conceive goals in ideal terms."[9] Local goal setting places the onus for their appropriateness upon local policymakers.

Variations in discretion affect the level of political interest in federal money allocations and the income groups that benefit.[10] When little discretion is accorded in spending, relatively few elected officials and interest groups are likely to be concerned about where funds are allocated. Decisions about federal funds, as a result, are likely to be made by program staff. If, on the other hand, large areas of a city are eligible to receive federal dollars, elected officials and interest groups are inclined to be more interested in how funds are spent. In such cases it is more likely that expenditure decisions will be made by elected officials and that benefits will be more widely dispersed than in instances of limited discretion. Fossett has noted a tendency for lower-income groups in fiscally hard-pressed cities to receive a smaller share of CDBG and CETA benefits than in more prosperous ones.[11] This tendency can be traced to the decisions of officials in struggling cities who, less constrained by regulations, had considerable incentives to use federal funds to support ongoing city services at politically acceptable levels. Greater political rewards are possible when funds are used as political resources and are more widely dispersed--rather than focused in the poorest areas.

When program objectives are not realized, one explanation is faulty implementation. Activities to be carried out were not executed or were subject to inordinate delays. Another explanation is that aspirations were too high. Studying the process of implementation, therefore, includes examining the setting of goals toward which implementation is directed.[12] The impact of the divergent goals for urban homesteading pursued in the subject cities will be discussed in a later chapter.

Incentives to Participants

The incentive of the Section 810 Program is the inventory of eligible, federally owned properties available for rehabilitation. Funds for program administration and rehabilitation loans and/or grants are not included. Whether cities choose to participate depends upon whether that incentive--along with the "minimal" strings attached to the program--outweighs the challenge of locating the requisite funds for administration and rehabilitation.

Derthick found that another major cause of the failure of the New Towns In-Town program was the limited supply of federal incentives. Known interchangeably as surplus lands for community development, Federal Lands for Critical Urban Needs, and New Towns In-Town, this federal initiative of the Johnson administration to build new communities on federally owned land in metropolitan areas has been labeled an unequivocal failure.[13]

The logic of the program was questioned as the federal government became unable to offer enough inducements of large, vacant tracts of land at low prices. Such land was limited, and there were legal objections to the original premise that surplus land be given away or sold cheaply. A belated discovery occurred: the sale of federal land at less than fair market value required a change in federal law. This change was not forthcoming.

Another cause of New Town In-Town failure was the federal government's limited ability to use such incentives as it possessed effectively. Because the program depended on local officials as the agents of its purpose, local liabilities became federal liabilities. Derthick found that local officials resisted federal direction: "Where little support existed, a directive from HUD to the mayor could not create it. Besides, the mayor would do what HUD asked only if he were eager to have its aid."[14]

Impact of Local Conditions

The literature supports the idea that local fiscal and political conditions will affect policy implementation. Pressman's conception of the power asymmetry between federal and local governments refutes the concept of cooperative federalism. "Cooperative federalism between relatively poor and powerless local agencies is an illusion," he wrote.[15]

The federal government generally insists on a range of guidelines and controls to accompany the financial benefits of grants-in-aid programs. A city faced with fiscal problems is weakly positioned to bargain about the conditions of a grant. The small scale of Urban Homesteading places cities in a less dependent position in relation to the program. However, faced with a range of housing problems, some urban areas apparently seize whatever small benefits are available.

Browning, Marshall, and Tabb suggest that nonstatutory variables--such as local political forces--may be more important to the success of policy implementation than the statutory variables emphasized by Sabatier and Mazmanian. A statute's strength influences implementation, and may be the only leverage point for national policymakers, but local factors can produce enormous variations in implementation.[16] Browning, Marshall, and Tabb concentrate on distributive policy aimed at changing the behavior of local government and emphasize micro-implementation by the subordinate or local government and a more detailed examination of variation among subunits. Their concern is how and whether variations in the strengths of Model Cities, general revenue sharing, and CDBG statutes shaped local implementation and effects from the perspective of minority interests. Findings from the Model Cities era suggest that federal programs have an important but limited capacity to influence the direction of political change.

In using Section 810, local officials used federal grants as leverage to pursue their own agendas. A city's use of new grant money depends partly on what it has done with previous revenue and the unfulfilled agendas of local actors.[17] The city tries to gather money from various sources to pursue those agendas. If federal funds limit the use of new money, other, more flexible funds, may be shifted to carry out the agendas.[18] Considering Model Cities a relatively strong statute, Browning, Marshall, and Tabb maintain that federal grants can change the odds of winning in the local policymaking process. Even with such strong statutory constraints, however, the ideology, interests, and agendas of local agents have a major impact on implementation.

Sabatier and Mazmanian contend that a well-drafted statute can provide officials with sufficient policy direction and legal resources to minimize the impact of short-term changes in public opinion and the capacity to bring about desired changes in widely different local jurisdictions. However, a contrary situation may also exist. For example, they find that policy outputs of implementing agencies are essentially a function of interaction between the legal structure and the political process. A statute with little institutionalized bias, therefore, leaves them very dependent upon variations in political support over time and among local settings.[19]

Local implementation is more subject to local input than from federal or other exogenous sources. Macro-implementation involves politics, and from outside.[20] Mutual adaptation typifies urban homesteading and is discussed later in this chapter.

More optimistic about the possibility of federal influence on local politics, Derthick states: "To achieve results, federal officials must have enough knowledge of local politics to perceive what incentives are necessary; they must supply the incentives in sufficient quantity; and they must direct the incentives to those holders of local power whose support is required to achieve the federal purpose. In short, they must intervene in local politics."[21] Derthick maintains this position despite the failure of New Towns In-Town. The design of the Urban Homesteading Program is a tacit endorsement of the internal adaptive process over the exercise of federal influence.

Mutual Adaptation Between Program Policy and Local Implementers

The fact that a federal program depends upon different local agencies necessitates some adjustments during implementation. Statutory provisions for such adjustments vary. The provision for local adaptation is an essential element of the Section 810 legislation.

Sundquist has observed that the dilemma of the federal system is the federal government's dependence upon the competence and motivation of state and local government officials whom it can influence and induce, but cannot directly control, to achieve national goals and objectives.[22] In the same vein, Derthick comments that when federal programs depend upon local political leaders, "whatever flaws are in the local officials' ability to act effectively--to gather support, to overcome opposition, to assemble an administrative organization--were liabilities for the federal government as well."[23]

Bardach's position on implementation differs subtly but significantly from the views of Derthick, Pressman, or Wildavsky. He disputes that implementation processes which lead to perversion or subversion of policy goals and to excessive financial costs are not explicitly identified and analyzed. He maintains that the character and degree of many implementation problems are inherently unpredictable. The classic symbols of underperformance, delay, and escalating costs are bound to appear even with the most robust policy--one that is well designed to survive the implementation process. He suggests that someone or some group must be willing and able to set a policy back on course. His case history of the implementation of legislation to restore the civil liberties of persons alleged to be mentally ill in California illustrates the point.

Variation in program implementation may be determined by circumstances of local priority and capacity to carry out a program. Robert Thomas has found that the way local officials determine the priority of a federal program is an integral part of the policy implementation process. Two key variables in priority setting are the deemed effectiveness of the program and the severity of the problem. In order for a federal program to attain priority on a local policy agenda and be adapted to local jurisdictions, area officials must determine that the program will effectively deal with problems, as they perceive them, without usurping their authority. An official would be reluctant to set a high priority for a federal project--regardless of how serious the problem--if it was thought that the program would be ineffective or in some way detrimental to his or her community or political situation. Federal program priority may be viewed as the relationship between officials' perceptions of problem severity and their assumptions about the effectiveness of a proposed plan of action. To be a high-priority item, a program must meet these criteria. Thomas has also found that, often, authorizations do not match appropriations. Federal agencies are thus deprived of one of the major tools to achieve state and local cooperation.

Thomas states that implementation must be conceptualized as a developmental process in order to understand how federal programs attain priority on the local policy agenda. "Federal programs are adapted to local circumstances," he comments, "through a complex policy process that operates to insure local integrity and participation in the application of federal programs."[24] Since federal programs do not have uniform consequences for diverse local conditions, they cannot be uniformly applied even when the intent is there. Federal administrators, as a result, must program objectives to accommodate divergent patterns of authority, varying local conditions, different abilities (expertise), and capabilities (resources)--as well as striving for political acceptance.

The use of persuasion and bargaining to induce parties to contribute to the program process is defined as a special breed of politics--implementation politics. Bardach has called it "a form of politics in which the very existence of an already defined policy mandate, legally and legitimately authorized in some prior political process, affects the strategy and tactics of the struggle." The politics of implementation are thus made highly defensive, resulting in a great deal of energy spent in maneuvering to avoid responsibility, scrutiny, and blame. Local implementation may become saddled with residual issues from the policymaking process. Or, as Bardach states, "Implementation is the continuation of politics by other means."[25]

Berman divides micro-implementation into three phases: mobilization, deliverer implementation, and institutionalization. Officials of the local organization decide about project adoption and plan for its execution in the mobilization phase. The term mobilization implies the crucial political and bureaucratic activities that are the real core of starting a new practice. The local organization's goals and agenda at the outset may profoundly affect the project's fate. If local priorities do not accord with those of the federal government, adaptation

decisions may be merely pro forma.[26] Berman classifies the
carrying out of local policy as deliverer implementation.
Implementation deliverers, as they translate the adopted
project or plan into an operational reality, repeatedly make
two kinds of decision: they choose to adapt project plans
to their standard behavior, or they adapt their behavior to
suit the plan.

CONCLUSION

     Federalism has traversed an erratic path toward
controlled decentralization. The enactment of Section 810
Urban Homesteading demonstrates ambiguity among federal
policymakers related to decentralization of control.
Establishment of a narrow-purpose categorical program in
1974 contradicted the trend toward broad-based programs such
as the CDBG. Urban homesteading, specific in some respects,
provides atypical flexibility as a categorical program. As
will be discussed, control over local implementors was an
essential element in Section 810 implementation and the
relationship between intergovernmental officials despite the
discretion afforded legislatively.
     Local implementation of federal programs manifests the
intergovernmental dilemma. The fundamental interdependence
among levels of government is common to federal domestic
programs. Beyond that, each program and each setting
possess unique circumstances that affect implementation.
The studies of implementation cited in this chapter provide
a useful theoretical framework for this study of Section 810
Urban Homesteading in: Baltimore, Detroit, and
Philadelphia.

NOTES

     1. Claude E. Barfield, Rethinking Federalism
(Washington, D.C.: American Enterprise Institute for Public
Policy Research, 1981).
     2. Lawrence D. Brown, James W. Fossett, and Kenneth T.
Palmer, The Changing Politics of Federal Grants (Washington,
D.C.: The Brookings Institution, 1984).
     3. Ibid., p. 15.
     4. George E. Hale and Marian Leif Palley, The Politics
of Federal Grants (Washington, D.C.: Congressional
Quarterly, 1981).
     5. Brown, Fossett, and Palmer, Changing Politics,
p. 11.
     6. Ibid. Changing Politics, p. 11.
     7. Hale and Palley, Politics of Federal Grants, p. 73.
     8. Jeffrey L. Pressman and Aaron Wildavsky,
Implementation (Berkeley and Los Angeles: University of
California Press, 1973).
     9. Martha Derthick, New Towns In-Town (Washington,
D.C.: The Urban Institute, 1972), p. 83.
     10. James W. Fossett, Federal Aid to Big Cities: The
Politics of Dependence (Washington, D.C.: The Brookings

Institution, 1983), p. 12.
    11. Ibid., pp. 46-48.
    12. Derthick, New Towns In-Town pp. xi-xii.
    13. Ibid., p. xiv.
    14. Ibid., p. 86.
    15. Jeffrey L. Pressman, Federal Programs and City Politics (Berkeley and Los Angeles: University of California Press, 1975), p. 12.
    16. Rufus Browning, Dale Marshall, and David Tabb, "Implementation and Social Change: Sources of Local Variation in Federal Social Programs," Policy Studies Journal 8 (1980):629.
    17. Ibid., p. 630.
    18. Ibid.
    19. Paul Sabatier and Daniel Mazmanian, "The Implementation of Public Policy: A Framework of Analysis," Policy Studies Journal 8 (1980):549.
    20. Paul Berman, "The Study of Macro- and Micro-Implementation," Public Policy 26 (Spring 1978):179.
    21. Derthick, New Towns In-Town, p. 84.
    22. James Sundquist, Making Federalism Work (Washington, D.C.: The Brookings Institution, 1969), p. 86.
    23. Derthick, New Towns In-Town, p. 86.
    24. Robert Thomas, "Implementing Federal Programs at the Local Level," Political Science Quarterly 94 (Fall 1979):422.
    25. Eugene Bardach, The Implementation Game, (Cambridge: MIT Press, 1977), p. 37.
    26. Berman, "Macro- and Micro-Implementation," p. 177. The literature suggests that the more discretion allowed and the fewer constraints imposed, the more an implemented program depends on the characteristics of the administering agencies.

3

Housing Policy Development
and Urban Homesteading

Section 810 Urban Homesteading is historically, legislatively, and fiscally related to other housing programs. Indeed, previous federal government housing policy has been charged with the blame for creating large inventories of vacant housing in cities that are the primary targets of urban homesteading programs. The philosophy of the urban homesteading concept can be illuminated by reviewing housing efforts that preceded it. This chapter chronicles the evolution of housing and community development policy.

Because Section 810 does not provide administrative and rehabilitation funds, program implementors must secure them from other sources. Community Development Block Grants have been the main source of funding for community development agencies in the three subject cities and elsewhere. Some of these funds have been diverted toward the administration of Section 810 Urban Homesteading and some rehabilitation loans and grants. Section 312 rehabilitation loans have likewise been a major source of support of Section 810 Urban Homesteading. Since urban homesteading substantially depends upon these two programs for its operation, brief descriptions of them are included in this chapter.

Federal involvement in housing and community development testifies to the need for intergovernmental cooperation in some areas. Sundquist has commented on the rapid movement toward the recognition of housing, health, welfare, and education as matters requiring a national solution that states and communities must carry out voluntarily or through more coercive means.[1] Legislative milestones have been the Housing Act of 1949, the Housing and Urban Development Act of 1965, and the Housing and Community Development Act of 1974. Significant thresholds in housing and community development programs occurred during the New Deal, Great Society, and New Federalism periods. These and other legislative actions will be briefly discussed.

EVOLUTION OF HOUSING AND COMMUNITY DEVELOPMENT POLICY

Until World War I, the federal government's involvement in housing and community development was limited to occasional studies and little else. In 1892, Congress commissioned a study for the investigation and documentation of slum conditions in four U.S. cities with populations over 200,000. Although the study found significant inadequacies in housing quality, no immediate action resulted.

Initial Inroads

In 1908, Theodore Roosevelt appointed a blue-ribbon panel--the President's Housing Commission--which innovatively recommended federal intervention in housing within the nation's major cities. The commission assessed the problems of slums in American cities, particularly on the Eastern Seaboard, where the worst neighborhoods had become the entry point for new immigrants. In an extensive report, the commission called for condemnation and wholesale federal purchase of slum properties--along with direct federal loans to finance construction of entire new sections of some cities--to enable the poor to buy or rent decent, sanitary housing at low interest rates or rents.[2] Congress did not respond to the commission's recommendations but did intervene on two other fronts in 1918. First, a loan program to realty companies was established for housing construction to aid shipyard families. Second, Congress created the U.S. Housing Corporation, which built and managed community projects for war workers near defense installations during and immediately after the war years.

Depression Era Efforts

Housing and community development benefited from the watershed of domestic policy during the Depression, when large-scale federal intervention in areas previously considered the province of the private sector began. President Herbert Hoover's Conference on Home Building and Home Ownership set the stage for subsequent reforms. The conference documented the nation's housing problems--ranging from local zoning deficiencies to the inadequate structure of the nation's thrift and construction finance institutions. A variety of finance-related housing and mortgage legislation was subsequently enacted between 1932 and 1937 including:

. Direct federal funding of low-income housing and slum clearance;
. Reorganization of the housing/thrift credit system to assist homeowners who could not otherwise obtain funds for housing;
. Emergency housing relief designed to refinance defaulted homeowner's mortgages and

> assist in the redemption of properties
> foreclosed because of mortgage nonpayment;
> . Creation of the federally chartered savings
>   and loan system;
> . Use of housing construction as a source of
>   emergency employment;
> . Creation of a low-rent public housing
>   program;
> . Passage of the National Housing Act of 1834,
>   intended to address the structure and
>   institutional inadequacies of the mortgage
>   market.[3]

Housing changes occurred as a consequence of the United States' entry into World War II. Servicemen and defense workers received housing assistance mortgage relief, Federal Housing Administration mortgage insurance for defense housing, and federal rent control. President Roosevelt created the National Housing Agency, which handled virtually all nonfarm housing programs. In 1942, it was replaced by the Housing and Home Finance Agency (HHFA), which remained the principal federal housing agency until the Department of Housing and Urban Development (HUD) was established in 1965.

A 1945 report of the Senate Committee on Postwar Economic Policy and Planning's Subcommittee on Housing and Urban Development called for legislation to provide an adequate housing supply. The panel recommended a national policy in which private enterprise was to meet the housing need for 1.2 million new units over the next ten years while government was restricted to a supplemental role. The subcommittee also recommended the creation of a permanent National Housing Agency.

The Housing Act of 1949 has been called the beginning of the modern era of federal housing and community development programs. It established a firm federal commitment to housing, declaring that

> the general welfare and security of the nation and
> the health and living standards of its people
> require housing production and related community
> development sufficient to remedy the serious
> housing shortage, the elimination of substandard
> and other inadequate housing through the clearance
> of slums and blighted areas, and the realization
> as soon as feasible of the goal of a decent home
> and suitable living environment for every American
> family.

The Urban Renewal component of the Housing Act (Title I) was far-reaching. As the program began to clear slums and run-down areas, businesses and residents had to relocate. Although this spawned new housing and commercial areas in some cities, large tracts of undeveloped vacant land resulted in others as redevelopment plans failed to materialize. Over three decades, the program became one of the most controversial in the history of federal housing and community development.

Urban Renewal

One distinctive element of housing and community development policy is the involvement of multiple interests and concerns in its implementation. Support for the Housing Act of 1949 came from widely dispersed quarters. Initially called "slum clearance," the 1954 law that broadened it referred to the program as "urban renewal." The legislation's language reflected divergent interests and emerged from the compromise of conflicting viewpoints. Some envisioned the legislation as a way to attract middle-income families and businesses back to the inner city. Some viewed it as a way to improve slum conditions and housing; others saw it as a means to enhance the quality of life in the inner city. Local government officials hoped to increase tax revenues, while some private investors anticipated a profitable real estate opportunity.

At the outset, the program's emphasis was on improving the central city tax base by attracting middle-class families and businesses back from the suburbs; the construction of public buildings and commercial centers was also stressed. The objective of redevelopment--to improve slum conditions and provide better housing for the poor--was virtually ignored. McFarland found that the need of federal leaders to sell the new program to mayors may have been one factor in the early thrust of this effort.[4] This appears to be an example of cooption by the federal government; localities were allowed to pursue their individual goals in order to garner the necessary local support to make the program work.

Policy in the 1950s and 1960s

The Housing Act of 1954 was a significant piece of legislation enacted after a 1953 report issued by President Eisenhower's Advisory Committee of Government Housing Policies and Programs. It called for federal aid to communities to combat the spread of slums; FHA financing for housing construction and rehabilitation in older urban areas; adaptation of FHA home mortgage programs to the special needs of low-income families; housing assistance for minority families; continuation of the public housing program; and creation of a private, secondary mortgage market. Specific measures were taken to prevent abuses in FHA programs.

Throughout the 1950s, housing and community development programs liberalized and expanded gradually to serve more special interest groups. Cooperative housing, college housing, and elderly housing benefited from new and/or expanded programs. The Housing Act of 1959, in particular, provided mortgage insurance to rental projects for the elderly and 3-percent loans for elderly rental housing developed by private nonprofit corporations.[5]

By the 1960s, the other side of urban renewal's conflicting objectives resurfaced: improvement of slum conditions as charges of wasteful spending, destruction of neighborhoods and small businesses, and eviction of poor

families took their toll. After President Kennedy appointed
Robert Weaver as HHFA administrator in 1961, steps were
taken to humanize the slum clearance program. Clearance
focused more on commercial and industrial sites and less on
residential neighborhoods.[6] More help was channeled into
finding decent homes for the displaced and easing their
transition to new locations. Reliance on the bulldozer
declined as more slum neighborhoods were scheduled for
rehabilitation to improve living conditions for residents.

Under the Kennedy administration, Congress rejected
efforts to establish a Cabinet-level department for housing
and urban concerns. The major piece of legislation enacted
at the time was the Housing Act of 1961, which made several
revisions to the urban renewal program. Among these changes
were increasing the federal share of program costs for
smaller cities and broadening the FHA 221 mortgage program
to cover all low- and moderate-income families, rather than
just displaced families. The act created a new rent subsidy
program to provide loans at rates as low as 3 percent to
nonprofit and limited dividend organizations, cooperatives,
and public bodies to finance projects for low- and moderate-
income families.

In 1964, during the Johnson administration, the Section
312 rehabilitation loan program initiated 3-percent
financing for housing and business property rehabilitation
in urban renewal or code enforcement areas and the expansion
of rural housing programs as part of the National Housing
Act. A major initiative of the Johnson administration was
passage of the Housing and Urban Development Act of 1965.
The act established the Department of Housing and Urban
Development (HUD) and transferred to it the functions of its
predecessor agencies: the Housing and Home Finance Agency,
the Federal Housing Administration, the Public Housing
Administration, and the Farmers Home Administration (FMHA).
Upon its creation, Congress declared that

> The general welfare and security of the Nation and
> the health and living standards of our people
> require, as a matter of national purpose, sound
> development of the Nation's communities and
> metropolitan areas in which the vast majority of
> its people live and work. To carry out such pur-
> pose, and in recognition of the increasing
> importance of housing and urban development in our
> national life, the Congress finds that estab-
> lishment of an executive department is desirable
> to achieve the best administration of the
> principal programs of the Federal Government which
> provide assistance for housing and for the
> development of the Nation's communities.

Nearly $8 billion in grants were authorized to pursue some
new directions in federal housing policy that established a
closer link between housing and urban renewal programs.

Model Cities

The next year saw the passage of the Demonstration
Cities and Metropolitan Development Act of 1966, commonly
known as the Model Cities Program. Mandating a coordinated
use of all available public and private resources, HUD
provided grants and technical assistance to help communities
plan and carry out concentrated and comprehensive
demonstration programs to rebuild and restore entire
sections or neighborhoods. A demonstration program was to
combine physical development and social programs to increase
the supply of lower-cost standard housing, alleviate social
problems, and contribute to a well-balanced city.
Model Cities was an innovative attempt to address
criticism of existing federal aid programs as "too small and
diffuse to have guided the process of urban development and
too much oriented to specific functions."[7] As a result of
the experience with Community Action Agencies (CAAs) set up
under the OEO in 1964 to wage the War on Poverty, HUD
officials emphasized the role of a city's own political
leaders to help implement federal aid programs. CAAs,
designed to coordinate federally aided social programs,
consisted primarily of program beneficiaries who often
became political adversaries of city hall and circumvented
local government officials. Their roles as coordinators of
federal programs in their communities were hence curtailed.
The original design of Model Cities to launch a massive
concentration of effort in the troubled neighborhoods of a
few cities vanished in the legislative process. The number
of eligible cities grew to a point where too little money
was available for too many cities (from a few to well over
100 ultimately). This political problem of targeting
efforts is one that has transcended the federal policymaking
level and also affects local policy implementation. The
program operated from 1966 to 1973.
Model Cities appropriations divided among dozens of
projects in each of 150 cities had only limited impact.
Much effort was spent to ensure citizen participation, often
at the expense of planning and cooperation of local units of
government. Model Cities was an important stepping-stone to
revenue sharing since it entailed fewer strings than other
urban programs. Decentralization was further promoted under
Nixon's administration and phased into the more general
package of urban development legislation.

Housing and Community Development Act of 1968

The Housing and Community Development Act of 1968 is
heralded as the most significant piece of housing
legislation passed during the 1960s. The act established a
national housing goal of 26 million new units over the next
ten years, including 6 million for low- and moderate-income
families and called for annual reports to Congress on
progress in meeting these goals. The act, through the
Section 235 home purchase subsidy program and the Section

236 rent subsidy program, respectively,   relied upon a new
technique of interest-subsidy payments in creating new
homeownership and rental programs for low- and moderate-
income families.   In Section 235, HUD made monthly payments
to lenders to reduce the borrower's effective rate on a
market-rate loan to as low as 1 percent.   The borrower paid
the greater of this subsidized rate or 25 percent of income.
Similarly, in the Section 236 program the tenant paid a
basic rent or 25 percent of income, whichever was greater,
not to exceed the market rent.   The market rent was based on
a market-rate mortgage and the basic rent was based on a
1-percent mortgage.
     Section 235 effectively increased the ability of city
out-migrants to sell their homes to low-income families.
The program artificially inflated inner-city property
values.   Shoddy workmanship, in some cases,   resulted in
major repair problems within short periods of occupancy.
Many new homeowners were not financially or technically
equipped to make necessary repairs.   In some instances,
homeowners faced with little equity--and no likelihood of
reselling at inflated prices--abandoned their properties.
     Among the reasons postulated for these problems were the
inherent flaws in the low-income homeownership concept; poor
administration of the program;   inadequate selection and
training of the participants;   and   external economic
conditions.   The ultimate result was that HUD became the
largest residential real estate owner and manager in the
country.[8] The programs lost much of their congressional
support as the news became widespread.   Innovative solutions
were continuously sought as the inventory of abandoned
houses--obtained through tax foreclosures by local
governments and through FHA foreclosures by the federal
government--grew.   Urban homesteading was one of the
solutions proposed in the early 1970s.
     Scandals broke out in the two major subsidized housing
programs (Section 235 and Section 236) even as urban renewal
and Model Cities came under attack.   Nixon imposed the
freeze on new commitments under these programs, in spite of
some objections,   during the period of congressional
indecisiveness that followed.

     Neighborhood Rehabilitation

     Disenchantment with the bulldozer approach to slum
improvement gave rise to an increased interest in
rehabilitation to improve slums and declining neighborhoods
in the 1960s.   Rehabilitation aims to improve neighborhoods
for poor residents and does not displace them as does
clearance.
     Slum clearance/urban renewal destroyed more homes than
it created.   By 1972--even with modifications proposed by
HHFA administrator Robert Weaver--just over 50 percent of
the units completed in urban renewal areas were for low- and
moderate-income families in contrast to only 39 percent five
years earlier.   Some improvements occurred in central cities

such as Baltimore's Charles Center, Philadelphia's Society
Hill, and Boston's Civic Center.   By the time the program
was suspended in 1974, HUD had approved $10 billion in
grants from over 2,000 urban renewal projects.   In view of
the magnitude of the central-city rebuilding job, however,
urban renewal did not have great impact.[9] It has been
suggested that the actions required to achieve urban renewal
goals proved to be mutually contradictory.   Improved results
may have been achieved with more flexibility and less
detailed review of local proposals: a better balance
between federal control and local discretion.
     Rehabilitating slum neighborhoods turned   out to be more
difficult than clearance   and rebuilding--a complicated
process itself.   It was also less glamorous.   Making
rehabilitation a reality took a lot of learning.   Several
early efforts were unsuccessful due to an underassessment of
what was required.
     The FHA conducted experiments during the mid-1960s to
learn how to include the rehabilitation of properties owned
by absentee landlords in decaying neighborhoods in several
cities.   Although all experiments were not successful, they
did yield a better understanding of urban decay and some
possible remedies.[10]
     If the success of residential rehabilitation is measured
not just by the number of units completed, but also by the
long-term improvement of housing, living, and neighborhood
conditions,   then   many   attempts   have   been   failures.[11]
Different approaches tried over time have not significantly
stemmed the tide of neighborhood decline.   Most recently,
various financing techniques and   other approaches are
employed in the many cities using block grants and low-
interest loans for rehabilitation.   Urban homesteading
efforts are among the innovative rehabilitation approaches
that HUD has mildly promoted using these two programs.

Policy in the 1970s

     By 1972,   there was general agreement that the urban
development programs needed revision.   Although it was a
generously funded and highly attractive "mayor's program" in
the 1950s and early 1960s, urban renewal had lost much of
its political appeal.   In Boston, New Haven, and elsewhere
political careers were launched with federal renewal
grants.[12] Nixon budget makers tightened federal controls as
evidence of local fiscal indiscipline--underbudgeting and
applications for large amendments--was revealed.   From the
local political perspective, urban renewal suffered an image
problem as it became known as "Negro removal."   The federal
government took steps to establish some protections, such as
the "one for one" rule requiring that a unit of public
housing for the poor be made available for every such unit
eliminated by a renewal project and a requirement that
relocation plans for those to be displaced be approved.
Activists among the urban poor were inclined and equipped to
block renewal plans.   Mayors who had comprised the main

constituency for urban renewal distanced themselves as
federal constraints, local opposition, and the program's
tainted reputation raised the political costs of renewal.

1974 Housing and Community Development Act

In January 1973 the Nixon administration placed a
moratorium on all subsidized housing programs, pending a
reevaluation of their effectiveness. This placed the Nixon
administration in a strong bargaining position when, later
that year, it insisted on changes in the pending 1974 CDBG
legislation as a precondition for restoring the flow of
funds.[13] The administration proposed that subsidized housing
activity be shifted to the leased housing program (Section
23). Under this program, private owners would lease new or
existing units to low-income tenants, who would pay 25
percent of their incomes for rent.

The 1974 Act created the CDBG Program by consolidating
seven previous categorical programs. The intent was to
broadly define objectives and eligible activities that allow
the local governments to design their own specific programs.
As originally conceived, larger cities and counties
automatically received funding through formulas while
smaller cities competed for discretionary funding from the
states and HUD. Entitlement communities participating in
the community development program were required to develop
housing assistance plans (HAPs), outlining needs and goals
for various types of low-income housing. The HAPs were to
be used by HUD in allocating subsidized housing
funds--providing a linkage between housing and community
development. The Housing and Community Development Act of
1974 created the Section 8 Program, patterned after Section
23. Under what became the major housing program of the
1970s and early 1980s, low- and moderate-income families
initially paid up to 25 percent (and later 30 percent) of
their income for rent, and HUD subsidized the difference
between that amount and the market rent. Fair market-rent
ceilings are established with the intent of controlling the
program cost.

Urban Development Action Grants

In 1977, Urban Development Action Grants (UDAGs) were
added to the community development program, providing
funding for specific projects in communities that met
minimum criteria for economic distress. Private financing
must be secured before a grant can be received by a city.
The UDAG Program can then provide the last component of
financing to make a project viable. UDAGs usually involve
large grants that cannot be underwritten from regular
community development funds. Action grants contribute to
industrial, commercial, and neighborhood development.
Through 1985, commercial projects accounted for 53 percent
of the grant awards; industrial projects for 25 percent; and
neighborhood projects for 22 percent.[14]

Gentrification

Gentrification of central city neighborhoods was a controversial issue during the most productive periods of urban homesteading implementation. Attracting upper-income households to the central city was a goal which could not be accomplished without some costs. Local governments would bear the criticism irrespective of the level of involvement when displacement occurred. The cities that directly encouraged and aided projects that promoted gentrification as well as those that did not have been targets of these charges.

The process of gentrification can be facilitated by local and federal urban homesteading government inducements. Besides the particular incentive of Section 810 property, homeownership is appealing due to policies that benefit all home buyers: income tax deductions. Other federally supported projects that inspire homeownership in revitalizing areas include credits for weatherization and the rehabilitation of historic structures.

Until the 1984 amendments to the Housing and Community Development Act, gentrifiers were in a superior financial position to partake of urban homesteading. The most obvious instance of gentrification supported by urban homesteading was found in Baltimore. The local program was utilized in a fashion consistent with stated local objectives to attract middle- and upper-income households to the central city. The Section 810 Program was not compatible with this objective. The eligible properties were not located in the downtown residential areas targeted in the city's revitalization strategy. Little, if any, displacement occurred as a direct result of urban homesteading in these areas.

Displacement of low-income persons without any relocation benefits or consideration is the most controversial aspect of gentrification. Both the occurrence of displacement and its propriety have been the subjects of debate. Nationwide, Section 810 was criticized for benefiting upper income groups, but little evidence existed to support this. Indeed the targeting of the program to lower-income families in Detroit probably impeded its output. The extent of displacement is greater than can be accounted for by urban homesteading.

Section 810 has limited capacity to contribute to gentrification and displacement due to program guidelines. Properties must be vacant prior to conveyance. Further, any household displaced as a consequence of this program would be eligible for relief under the Uniform Relocation Assistance and Real Property Acquisition Policies Act of 1970. Displacement data on urban homesteading programs is meager, but its greatest potential for displacement would be indirect, that is, resulting from spin-off activities in surrounding communities. This is ironic, since the success of urban homesteading as a neighborhood revitalization tool depends on the extent to which housing demand and/or maintenance is either revived or sustained.

The Department of Housing and Urban Development undertook a study of displacement in urban homesteading neighborhoods after two years of operation. No subsequent effort has been made to assess its impact. The analysis of data from forty neighborhoods in twenty-three demonstration cities concluded that owner-occupants in urban homesteading neighborhoods had not been victims of displacement. The initial data also suggested that, contrary to revitalization during its early stages, urban homesteading had either a contrary or no effect. Owners moving out were replaced by households with significantly lower (22 percent) incomes, suggesting continuation of decline rather than replacement.

Contrary to earlier HUD reports that no more than 100 to 200 households were displaced annually, more current studies now gauge total annual displacement in the United States at approximately 2.5 million persons.[15] Another contradiction to conventional thinking finds that displaced outmovers are not primarily poor or blue-collar, minority households. First generation gentrification affects primarily white, lower to middle income, socially heterogeneous neighborhoods.[16] Additional research is needed to determine the contribution of urban homesteading programs to these figures. The scope of the Section 810 program makes it unlikely that such research will be initiated or that any significant effects will be noted.

Community Development Block Grant Program

The existing special purpose or categorical grants subsumed in the CDBG legislation were: (1) urban renewal, (2) the neighborhood development program, (3) Model Cities, (4) water and sewer projects, (5) neighborhood facilities, (6) open space, and (7) loans for public facilities. Model Cities and urban renewal projects comprised 90 percent of the funds consolidated in the CDBG Program. In this process seven specific objectives were encompassed into one broad primary objective.

Three fundamental changes in urban aid embodied in the block grant approach of the 1974 Housing and Community Development Act were:

1. Attachment of fewer strings. Advance applications were not required for each project undertaken. Recipient communities developed their own programs and funding priorities. They were required to report to HUD only after decisions were made and funds obligated.

2. The amount of funds allocated to each governmental unit that applied was calculated based on a formula. The amount given to each unit of government was determined chiefly by the formula, without regard for the merits of

specific local projects (as had been the case in the past).

3. The block grant could cover 100 percent of the cost of any project chosen. Previous programs usually required the locality to cover some portion of the project cost.

The rationale for CDBG was based in part upon the belief that decentralization of government is desirable. The elimination of red tape and the lengthy processing delays required in numerous categorical grant programs was another reason. Statutorily, all CDBG activities must benefit either low- or moderate-income persons; aid in preventing and eliminating slums and blight; or address other community development issues that present a serious and immediate threat to a community's health and welfare. A chief criticism of the program has been the diversion of funds away from low-income to middle-income areas. A HUD-commissioned report by the National Association of Housing and Redevelopment Officials, which monitored the program, indeed found a shift of activities from lower-income to middle-income parts of the city.[17] Another concern has been that national goals would be accorded a much lower priority on local scales under block grants.

Opponents of block grants questioned whether local governments could resist local political pressures, which are strongest from those who need help least and weakest from those who need help the most. It was thought that the block grant approach might defeat the national goals and social priorities reflected in federal legislation. In some cases block grant money was not targeted and indeed went to areas least in need. This pattern supports the contention that local discretion in implementation does deviate from the goals of federally legislated programs.

Changes to the original CDBG legislation reflect criticisms and observations made during its original program years. New formulas for the distribution of funds were adopted to provide greater assistance to older central cities declining because of loss of population and business. Greater emphasis was placed on the use of funds primarily to meet the needs of low- and moderate-income families. Current regulations specify that no less than 51 percent of the funds received must be used for activities that benefit low- and moderate-income persons, over a period specified by the grantee, but not to exceed three years. In addition, the UDAG program--which authorizes a multi-year commitment of funds toward the revitalization of a specific distressed neighborhood--was established. And finally, legislative changes encouraged more attention to the rehabilitation of deteriorated housing and the revitalization of distressed slum neighborhoods.

These changes may at least partially explain the dispositions of CDBG participants in a Brookings Institution study of the use of Community Development Act funds in sixty-one cities.[18] In the first two years of the program

(1975-76)   officials in only   sixteen jurisdictions believed
that HUD had a major or determining influence on the content
of their community development programs.   In 1977, however,
officials in almost half of the jurisdictions (twenty-seven
cities) thought that HUD's role had expanded; and in 1978,
again about half (thirty-one cities) responded the same way.
     The increasing congressional interest in rehabilitation
is evident in CDBG legislative changes.   In the original
legislation,   block   grant funds could be   applied to
rehabilitation only if it was incidental to other activities
in a particular neighborhood.   The 1977 amendments gave
credence to rehabilitation as an independent,   eligible
activity. This reflected the use of CDBG funds at the local
level as a major resource for neighborhood rehabilitation
and revitalization.

     Section 312 Rehabilitation Loan Program

     Section 312 of the Housing Act of 1964,   as amended,
provides funds to   localities to   make loans   for the
rehabilitation of single- and multi-family residential
properties and nonresidential properties. Loans can only be
made in areas where the rehabilitation is a part of a CDBG
project or other designated area (such as urban renewal,
urban homesteading, or code enforcement).
     Federal regulations requiring   the concentration of
Section 312 loans in urban homesteading areas to support the
rehabilitation of single-family properties began in fiscal
year 1981.   The funds are distributed to localities with
approved Urban Homesteading programs, based upon need and
past use of Section 312 funds to assist the programs.   In
fiscal year 1982,   Section 312 loans comprised a larger
portion in rehabilitation financing for urban homesteading
than in 1981.[19] In total, 502 loans amounting to $9.259
million were provided in urban homesteading during fiscal
year 1982, compared to 281 loans totalling $5.216 million
provided during fiscal year 1981.   Three-quarters of the
rehabilitation financing provided for Section 810 during
1985 came from Section 312.[20]
     At present federal rules require that loans may not
exceed $27,000 per dwelling unit to raise the property to
the applicable local building code,   project,   or plan
standards.   Local governments can establish different loan
limits within the federal guidelines.   Loans for single-
family housing loans are repayable over twenty years at
interest rates of 3 to 9 percent, based upon family income.
Originally, the interest rate was a flat 3 percent but was
changed to variable rates in 1982.   An interest rate of 3
percent is charged to low- and moderate-income borrowers.
Low- and moderate-income, as defined by the 1978 amendments
to the Housing and Community Development Act of 1974, means
income which does not exceed 95 percent of the area median
income.   Before October 1978, the term meant not to exceed
80 percent of the area median income.   Higher income refers
to those whose income exceeds that of low- and moderate-
income property owners. HUD requires that priority be given

to low- and moderate-income homeowners but does not specify
the terms of such priority.   Community rehabilitation
officials interviewed by the General Accounting Office (GAO)
differed in their interpretations of priority. As a result,
the benefits accorded to low- and moderate-income homeowners
varied considerably from community to community.[21]
     There are no applicant income requirements maintained
nationwide. Participating communities can set such criteria
independently.   Detroit set low/moderate income standards
for this program; Baltimore did not; Philadelphia adopted
them after a few years.   Hence, neither Section 312 nor
urban homesteading legislation established clear guidelines
for implementing the priority provision.   Communities have
interpreted it for themselves.
     Interpretation of local administrators and HUD officials
vary but fall into three general categories.

>   1.   Those who say federal priorities are met if a
>   least 50 percent of the Section 312 loans or
>   funds are awarded to low- and moderate-income
>   families.
>   2.   Those who give priority by restricting loans
>   to applicants from low- and moderate-income
>   target neighborhoods, regardless of personal
>   income.
>   3.   Those who grant priority by restricting loans
>   exclusively to lower-income families.[22]

Urban Homesteading: A Solution?

     Urban homesteading attempted to address the problem of
abandonment that had developed over a considerable period of
time.   As a federal program, it followed on the heels of
many others that aimed to provide safe,   decent, sanitary
housing for all Americans. The limited scope of Urban
homesteading, due to program guidelines, dictates that it
can make only a small contribution toward resolving this
problem.
     Urban homesteading reflects legislative trends observed
in the roster of housing programs.   One is the emphasis on
comprehensiveness and   coordination of   efforts.   This
arrangement is inevitable for urban homesteading in those
cities where it depends on CDBG and Section 312 for funds.
It also means that urban homesteading is subject to rules
associated with those programs.   The impact of this
relationship will be elucidated in a later chapter.   The
second trend is the tenuous means by which low- and
moderate-income housing needs are addressed.   During some
periods,   they were acknowledged--but ignored.   During
others, efforts were made: but without consistency.   When
regulatory slack existed, emphasis shifted away from this
group.   The Section 810 regulations, without firm income
stipulations, did not focus on the housing needs of low- and
moderate-income persons.

NOTES

1. James Sundquist, Making Federalism Work (Washington, D.C.: The Brookings Institution, 1969), p. 11.

2. Barry G. Jacobs, Guide to Federal Housing Programs (Washington, D.C.: The Bureau of National Affairs, 1982), p. 3.

3. Ibid., pp. 12-13.

4. M. Carter McFarland, The Federal Government and Urban Problems (Boulder, Colorado: Westview Press, 1978), p. 77.

5. Jacobs, Guide to Federal Programs, p. 15.

6. McFarland, Federal Government and Urban Problems, p. 77.

7. George E. Hale and Marian Leif Palley, The Politics of Federal Grants (Washington, D.C.: Congressional Quarterly, 1981), p. 13.

8. HUD, Evaluation of the Urban Homesteading Demonstration Program: Final Report. 5 vols. (Washington, D.C.: GPO, 1981), vol. 2, p. 10.

9. McFarland, Federal Government and Urban Problems, p. 78.

10. Ibid., p. 80.

11. Ibid., pp. 80-81.

12. Lawrence D. Brown, "Politics of Devolution," in Lawrence D. Brown, James W. Fossett, and Kenneth T. Palmer, The Changing Politics of Federal Grants (Washington, D.C.: The Brookings Institution, 1984), p. 70.

13. Ibid., p. 72.

14. HUD 1986 Consolidated Annual Report to Congress on Community Development Programs (Washington, D.C.: GPO, 1986), pp. 68-69. Neighborhood projects usually involve housing, but they can also be commercial or industrial, depending on focus: neighborhood revitalization or employment opportunities for neighborhood residents.

15. Richard T. LeGates and Chester Hartman, "The Anatomy of Displacement in the U.S.," in Neil Smith and Peter Williams, eds., Gentrification of the City (Boston, Massachusetts: Allen & Unwin, 1986), p. 197.

16. Ibid., p. 198.

17. McFarland, Federal Government and Urban Problems, p. 74.

18. Paul R. Dommel, J. S. Hall, V. E. Bach, L. Rubinowitz, L. L. Haley, and J. S. Jackson, III, Decentralizing Urban Policy, (Washington, D.C.: The Brookings Institution, 1982), p. 69; Dommel, in Brown, Fossett, and Palmer, Changing Politics, p. 39.

19. HUD, 1983 Consolidated Annual Report to Congress on Community Development Programs (Washington, D.C.: GPO, 1983), p. 127.

20. HUD, 1986 Consolidated Annual Report to Congress, p. 110.

21. GAO, Report to the Congress of the United States; Urban Homesteading: A Good Program Needing Improvement (Washington, D.C.: GPO, 1979).

22. Ibid.

4

Development of Urban Homesteading: Origin and Operation

The federal government has periodically used homesteading to redistribute population to areas unable to attract a significant number of residents--either because of remote location or other disincentive pressures. The legislative origin of urban homesteading can be traced back to May 20, 1862, when President Lincoln signed the first homesteading act. Under the provisions of the Homestead Act, applicants received grants of 80 to 160 acres of land (depending on location) to improve and make their permanent residence for five years. The offer of free land, while popular, was criticized for not ending government sales of land or providing effective protection against speculation. Another complaint was that the government's policy of land grants for railroads and other improvements removed the best land from the public domain. To improve the economic vitality and encourage settlement of the arid West, Congress amended the act to allow for 320-acre and 640-acre grants. Legislation in 1912 reduced the residency requirement from five years to three years to improve the odds for homesteaders. Gradually, frontier homesteading became less attractive economically; the practical end occurred in the 1930s when most of the remaining public land was withdrawn from homesteading eligibility. Homesteading under this legislation did continue in Alaska until 1984.[1]

A second major homesteading attempt occurred with the passage of the National Industrial Recovery Act of 1933. It incorporated the subsistence homestead concept intended to rectify the population concentration in industrial centers. The newly created Division of Subsistence Households in the Department of the Interior implemented the program. The New Deal subsistence homestead program emphasized the creation of cooperative communities. A number of problems arose, including cost overruns and lack of a sound economic base in most communities. New initiatives were abandoned in 1937 after several changes in the program's administrative authority led to changes in direction.[2]

Local governments began applying the concept of urban homesteading in 1973. Wilmington, Delaware, closely followed by Baltimore and Philadelphia, was the first city to operate a locally legislated program. Such programs attracted substantial positive publicity. By the mid-1970s, between twelve and fifteen cities had begun some semblance of an urban homesteading program.   The actual number is difficult to   determine because   some programs   called homesteading were more like traditional means of disposing of foreclosed properties--with the possible addition of new public relations efforts.   Early initiatives testify to the strong appeal of urban homesteading to local governments.[3] Local urban homesteading provided a partial solution to the problems caused by abandoned and deteriorated housing, while providing homeownership opportunities.

In the beginning,   urban homesteading was   invariably equated with the process of homesteading that settled the American frontier.   Much   of   the   initial support and attention for urban homesteading can be traced to this analogy. But criticism also arose, from those who found the 160 acres   offered under   the Rural   Homesteading Act economically feasible,   unlike "urban homesteading which offers a shell of a dwelling with no real economic value."[4] Such a reaction does not take into account that both attempted to promote social goals by granting real property. Settlers and homesteaders shared similar commitments.   The land granted to them required years of toil and a large investment of capital before it could support a family.[5]

Modern Conceptualization

Urban homesteading was first proposed in the late 1960s as a way to address the pervasive problem of housing abandonment.   By   1970,   mention of the   term "urban homesteading" as a solution had become widespread.   The actual causes of abandonment are varied and interrelated; however, several major factors have been identified. Beginning in the 1960s population movement away from central cities was accompanied by employment and transportation trends that diminished the appeal of urban neighborhoods. Larger proportions of lower-income residents remained in such neighborhoods in the wake of   middle-class out-migration.   Higher property taxes,   increasingly unmet demands for governmental services,   and other factors depressed urban residential property values.   Financial institutions reacted by withholding   mortgage money in central cities; this reduced the number of home sales. Some homeowners, faced with no prospective buyers, walked away from their properties--leaving them for eventual government acquisition.

The extent to which urban homesteading can ameliorate abandonment is directly related to the pool of available properties.   In 1974, HUD's national inventory reached its high point of 75,000 properties. The agency--the largest single landlord nationally--held only a small fraction of the abandoned houses in most cities.   Most HUD-owned abandoned properties were concentrated in northeastern cities.   Municipal governments held large numbers of tax-delinquent properties,   but the   largest reservoir was

believed to be made up of privately owned abandoned
properties. Philadelphia and Detroit each had estimated
abandonment levels of 25,000 in 1974, and national estimates
of single-family abandonment ran as high as 300,000. The
maximum number of HUD-vacant properties reached over 16,000
in Detroit and 8,000 in Philadelphia during the 1970s.
During the 1970s, Baltimore had a maximum of 168 HUD-vacant
properties, while the sum of all vacancies reached as high
as 17,700 during the 1970s. It became apparent that urban
homesteading, to help local governments combat abandonment,
must be able to draw properties from sources other than the
HUD inventory.[6] In 1979, the federal government's first
effort to increase the pool of available properties
occurred: the addition of Veterans Administration (VA) and
Farmers Home Administration (FmHA) houses as eligible urban
homesteading properties.

Few labored under the delusion that urban homesteading
was a cure-all for the problem of housing abandonment.
Public statements and analyses in the press emphasized that
urban homesteading could be useful if carefully applied
under special circumstances.

LEGISLATIVE HISTORY

Cities as Urban Laboratories

The federal government attempted an intermediate step to
support local urban homesteading before creating Section
810. In early 1974, HUD, under the Property Release Option
Program (PROP), made 4,100 houses available to 43 cities for
use in urban homesteading or other public purposes.

According to administrative rules, houses supplied under
PROP could not have any remaining property value. Some
cities refused to accept any such properties, due to their
poor condition, or demolished them for parks and open space
rather than homestead them. Cities were reluctant to place
homesteaders in severely damaged properties where repair
costs would exceed the probable market value of the
rehabilitated residence. In some cases the value of houses
in good condition was questionable because of the
deteriorated surrounding neighborhoods. As it turned out,
PROP was an incremental step toward greater involvement by
the federal government in homesteading.[7]

The problems encountered by early local government
homesteading programs suggested federal legislation as the
next logical step in the evolution of homesteading.
National attention aroused sufficient interest in the
concept in spite of (and, to some extent, because of)
problems faced by cities. Cities experienced particular
difficulty in selecting low-income households for
participation, due to the high rehabilitation costs of
available sites and the lack of rehabilitation financing.
HUD possessed properties in better condition than the low-
value PROP structures and had existing programs for

rehabilitation financing and neighborhood improvement that could be adapted to meet the need of homesteading.[8]

The adoption of federal legislation had several consequences. It provided an additional source of vacant properties: those held in the HUD inventory. It served as an inducement for additional cities to participate in the program. It expanded the scope of the experiment in the application of the urban homesteading concept. And gradual inclusion of other eligible property (VA, FmHA, locally owned) among those available for Section 810 acquisition broadened the base of the experiment even further.

Federal Enactment

Congressional interest in local homesteading initiatives yielded the first proposal for federal legislation in late 1973. Submitted by Representative Marjorie S. Holt of Maryland, the National Homestead Act of 1973 proposed the homesteading of HUD-owned, deserted single-family housing units to combat the severe problem of abandonment and to encourage private homeownership.[9]

Molly Beals Millman found the legislative history of the federal urban homesteading program to be remarkably brief.[10] The concept attracted a broad base of political support, and little substantive opposition. The program was enacted into law less than a year after the first legislative proposal. The provisions proposed in the Senate version were essentially those adopted. Proposed by Senator Joseph Biden of Delaware, a liberal Democrat, the bill gave local and state governments more authority and autonomy than the Holt bill. Federally owned properties would be transferred to a local public agency rather than directly to a homesteader as Holt's bill required. Local governments would establish procedures for selecting homesteaders, based upon their need for housing and ability to make or cause to be made the necessary repairs within eighteen months to meet local codes. Three years was the minimum residency requirement. The bill required local communities to conduct a coordinated approach toward neighborhood renewal through the homesteading program and upgrading of community-service facilities. Under an expansion of the Section 312 provisions of the Housing Act of 1964, homesteaders could obtain low-interest rehabilitation loans from the federal government. HUD was to provide local governments with lists of all unoccupied one- to four-family structures on request. Passage of the other complex and controversial legislation comprising the Housing and Community Development Act of 1974 overshadowed Section 810, which approved urban homesteading.

The goals of the program remain the same: (1) to utilize existing housing stock; (2) to upgrade neighborhood facilities and services that will encourage more public/private investment; and (3) to provide homeownership opportunities. The localities develop goals and practical applications of the program within this framework. A community's objectives--whether they are preventing displacement, fighting abandonment, or revitalizing

neighborhoods--dictate design alternatives such as selection
of homesteaders, methods of financing, or methods of
rehabilitation.[11]

Section 810 of the Housing and Community Development Act
of 1974 authorized the Federal Urban Homesteading Program as
a demonstration project. Operations began in twenty-three
demonstration cities in fall 1975. HUD selected sixteen
additional cities to participate in the second round of
demonstration cities in May 1977. HUD's charged its Office
of Policy Development and Research with administering the
urban homesteading demonstration program in May 1975 and
conducting an evaluation three years from the date of
enactment. Cities were required to submit program proposals
to HUD with a homesteading plan designed to meet their
particular needs and effectively utilize their available
resources. The invitation to participate contained a
minimum number of constraints and requirements to maintain
the emphasis upon local initiative. An overwhelming
response to the invitation resulted. This response, coupled
with the existence of fewer properties than anticipated
within the target neighborhoods, enabled HUD to choose
twenty-three demonstration cities rather than the original
ten and still remain within the $5 million authorization.
The evaluation report contained findings and recommendations
for future use of the program. The demonstration's
preliminary results were encouraging enough for HUD to
announce its succession to operating status in September
1977. When final guidelines were published in December
1978, it became a fully operational program. While the
transfer of status did not substantially change the focus or
administrative approach developed in the demonstration
program, fluctuations in support at the national and local
levels have occurred. Criticism from those persons with
unfulfilled expectations began to accompany support of urban
homesteading. Nonetheless, by 1983, 110 cities and 12
counties had participated.

When urban homesteading became a full-fledged operating
program, HUD shifted responsibility for its administration
from the Office of Policy Development and Research to the
Office of Community Planning and Development. In the four
years under Policy Development and Research, timely annual
reports had been prepared as well as a five-volume
evaluation of the overall demonstration effort, as required
by law. During the next two years, however, no annual
reports appeared. That awkward transition was just one sign
of the periodic, waning support of urban homesteading at the
national level.

The urban homesteading staffing assignment at HUD
headquarters experienced a major change in late 1984, when
urban homesteading was redesignated as a division (after
having operated somewhat innocuously as another rehabilitation program) with a newly appointed director, two
professional staff people, and an administrative assistant.

Fiscal support of urban homesteading has been
inconsistent. Between 1975 and 1980, Congress appropriated
$55 million for the acquisition of urban homesteading

properties.   Between 1980 and 1982,   no   appropriations
occurred.   (See   Table   4.1 for   legislative/program
milestones.)   Unused appropriations were sufficient to
operate the program in 1982 at a level comparable to
previous years.   HUD staffers   attribute the apparent
slowdown to the start-up time required for programs to
become functional.   Derthick and others might similarly
attribute it to the front-end demands of adapting a new
program to local conditions.

PROGRAM MECHANICS

   Federal Administration

   The HUD area managers are responsible for the management
of urban homesteading programs within their respective
jurisdictions.   This authority is handed down from the HUD
headquarters through the regional office to the field office
and,   finally,   to   the   area office.   Interaction, then,
between program implementors and national officials occurs
mainly at the local level.   Among the specific charges of
the area manager are:

   1. The final approval of applications;
   2. The reservation of Section 312 rehabilitation
       and Section 810 funds;
   3. The signing of Urban Homesteading agreements;
   4. The   renewal   and/or amendment   of   Urban
       Homesteading agreements;
   5. The provision of lists of HUD-owned properties
       requested by the locality;
   6. The determination of the fair market value of
       each property to be transferred.

   After the local Urban Homesteading Program is approved,
the area manager executes an agreement with the unit of
government.   The agreement reserves Section 810 funds, on
behalf of the locality, for a twelve-month program year.
These funds are available for localities to reimburse the
FHA or other insurance fund for the fair market value of the
properties they select.   The HUD manager allocates the 810
funds to localities, based upon the estimated value of the
requested properties and the availability of funds.
   The Section 810 Urban Homesteading Program   is a
categorical program that requires each locality to apply for
participation in a competitive process.   The application
must include the designation of urban homesteading neighborhoods.   Cities also must demonstrate that HUD-owned
vacant properties are contributing to the decline of such
neighborhoods.   In selecting property, cities consider its
location, condition,   and capacity to further local revitalization and stabilization efforts.   Selected federally
owned properties are transferred to local governments with
HUD-approved urban homesteading neighborhoods.   The pot of
Section 810 funds reimburse federal agencies for the Section

810 value of the transferred properties. The city's allocation is reduced by that amount for the transferred property.[12] Local governments, in turn, transfer the properties to eligible households for a nominal sum. The homesteading is subject to certain repair and occupancy time limitations. Under the rules and regulations of the operating program, $15,000 was the maximum value of a single family house and $5,000 the maximum allowed for each additional unit up to the maximum of four. In 1984 the base limitation was raised to $20,000.

Both the federal and local government have roles in administering the Section 810 Urban Homesteading Program. The federal role is intended to be minimal, as provided for in the general program guidelines. While possibly maintaining a low level of intervention, the federal dicta inevitably provide the context within which local discretion is exercised.

Local Administration

Under federal urban homesteading legislation, no funds are made directly available for the local administration of the program or for the rehabilitation of properties. The responsibility of cities to finance administrative costs was a prominent issue in some early debates over participation.[13] Logically, the issue of administrative funding could impose constraints on program design and implementation. During the demonstration period, the cost of local administration grew from a median of $55,000 the first year to $85,000 the second year and $103,000 for the third year.[14] A wide variation in administrative costs existed throughout the demonstration, primarily reflecting differences in program scope and staffing. Personnel costs during the third year ranged from $18,000 to $160,000; total operating costs ranged from $33,000 to $210,000. Though not documented, these trends could be expected to continue.

Most local governments used CDBG funds to cover Section 810 administrative costs. Discretion allowed in the expenditure of CDBG funds and the federal government's emphasis upon a "coordinated approach" with other neighborhood improvement efforts makes this an attractive means of funding urban homesteading. In addition to supporting program administration, CDBG funds have been used by local urban homesteading communities to acquire local properties for homesteading; to provide direct grants and loans to homesteaders; and to leverage loans from private sources. For fiscal and programmatic reasons, staff within implementing agencies frequently shared responsibilities for urban homesteading and other programs.

Functions in the management of a local urban homesteading program fall into three basic areas: legal, operational, and support services. While the administrative functions are usually consolidated in one agency, it is possible--in an alternative arrangement--for several agencies to work in concert to provide them. In the Urban

TABLE 4.1
LEGISLATIVE/PROGRAM MILESTONES
SECTION 810 URBAN HOMESTEADING

DATE	MILESTONE
August 1974	Housing and Community Development Act becomes law. Public Law 93-383 authorizes $5 million to urban homesteading for FY 1976.
October 1975	HUD selects 23 first round urban homesteading demonstration cities.
December 1975	First properties are transferred from HUD to demonstration cities.
FY 1977	$5 million appropriated to urban homesteading.
May 1977	Selection of 16 second round demonstration cities. $15 million appropriated to urban homesteading.
June 1978	HUD announces the redelegation of authority to approve new urban homesteading applications to HUD area managers under the supervision of regional administrators.
FY 1978	$15 million appropriated to urban homesteading.
December 1978	Status of urban demonstration converted from demonstration to operating program.
FY 1979	$20 million appropriated to urban homesteading.
1979	Housing and Community Development Amendments of 1979 provide for reimbursement by HUD to the Veteran's Administration (for VA-owned properties) and to the Farmer's Home Administration (for FMHA-owned properties) conveyed to local urban homesteading agencies.
FY 1982	$10.1 million appropriated to urban homesteading.
1982	HUD concentrated all Section 312 rehabilitation loans for single-family homes in HUD-approved urban homesteading areas.

44

FY 1983 1983	$12 million appropriated to urban homesteading. The Housing and Urban-Rural Recovery Act of 1983 changes urban homesteading time-frames for rehabilitation and occupancy, gives priority to lower-income families, promotes sweat equity, and increases maximum allowable acquisition cost from $15,000 to $20,000.
FY 1984	$12 million appropriated to urban homesteading.
FY 1985 1985	$12 million appropriated to urban homesteading. Revised regulations took effect to implement provisions of the Housing and Urban-Rural Recovery Act of 1983; to simplify urban homesteading neighborhood designation, and for stronger program monitoring and compliance. Congress appropriates $12 million for FY 1985.
FY 1986	$12 million appropriated to urban homesteading.
FY 1987	$12 million appropriated to urban homesteading
FY 1988	$14.4 million appropriated to urban homesteading.

(Compiled by author.)

Homesteading Demonstration, it was determined that, in most cases, the division of administrative responsibilities reflected differences in the structure of the local government, staff or local statutes, financial resources, and staff expertise.[15] Legal responsibility is assumed by the signatory to the Urban Homesteading Agreement, but the daily operations may be managed by another agency.

Local units of government are able to select the operating agency for their respective Urban Homesteading Programs within the framework of the federal guidelines. The agency so designated usually is either an existing city government department, an independent public organization such as local development authority or housing commission, or a nonprofit, housing-oriented organization. This is in keeping with program guidelines, which indicate that a nonprofit agency, a local development corporation, or a neighborhood nonprofit organization can run the program. The choice of agency tends to reflect local assessments of organizational capacity as well as legal status--such as the authority to accept properties transferred by the federal government and to convey them to homesteaders. In fact, some demonstration cities designated one public entity to sign the Urban Homesteading Agreement with HUD, but designated or established another separate agency to manage daily operations. The demonstration program evaluation mentioned differences in the structure of local government, state or local statutes, financial resources, and staff expertise as key issues in the division of responsibilities. Property selection, homesteader selection, arrangement of financing, and planning and management of rehabilitation were the basic, necessary functions undertaken in all programs. (See the prototypical model.)

Initially, HUD provided no guidelines for the determination of need or the setting of income limits. Local governments were to consider two factors in selecting homesteaders: the prospective recipient's need for housing and his or her capacity to make or cause to be made the required repairs and improvements. The actual rehabilitation could be carried out by a contractor or by the homesteader. During the process, the homesteader might be required to permit inspections of the property and the rehabilitation work performed. The homesteader ultimately receives title to the property when the requirements have been met.

Variation among participating cities can be expected within these parameters. The demonstration program evaluation found that the emphasis on local input led to great diversity in program design and intent. Further, the local programs varied in their approach to and sequencing of necessary functions. Variations reflect both practical realities--available staff, financing options, and the number and condition of candidate properties in the HUD inventory--as well as policy considerations like the relative emphasis on self-help as opposed to contracted repairs, the level of agency involvement in the homesteading process, and the target homesteader population.[16] Individual

Figure 4.1
Prototypical Urban Homesteading Model

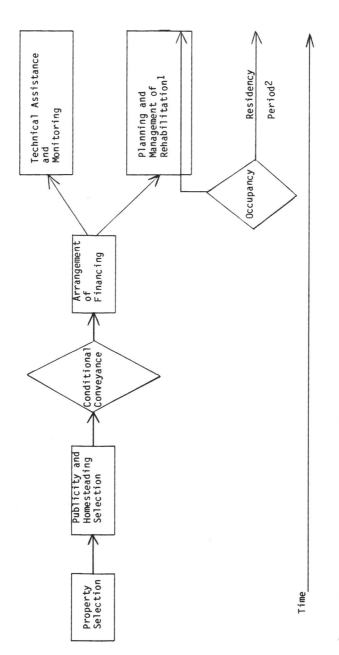

[1]Time allowed for completion of rehabilitation was extended from 18 to 36 months by the Housing and Urban-Renewal Recovery Act of 1983.

[2]Length of required residence extended from 3 to 5 years by the Housing and Urban-Renewal Recovery Act of 1983.

programs could be expected to take on various forms in
addressing these factors.

Considerable variation in the sequencing and time
allotted for each task occurred in the demonstration. The
decisions basically determined the amount of control given
to the homesteader or the agency staff. The model of the
urban homesteading process greatly simplifies how the
process actually takes place. The sequence is rarely so
linear or the tasks so discrete.[17] More often, the agency
performs several functions simultaneously, and the outcome
of one phase directly affects the timing or scope of the
next.

Three milestones are included in sequencing. Local
administrators can alter the time required to complete the
homesteading path by modifying, within Section 810
guidelines, the deadlines for conveyance (from federal
agency to local agency to homesteader), occupancy, and
completion of rehabilitation. Variations among localities
had little impact on program outcomes.

Rehabilitation is generally a staff-intensive endeavor.
Substantial staff commitments are required in order to
administer an Urban Homesteading Program; involvement is
required from the original screening of applications to the
final conveyance some years hence, as illustrated in Figure
4-1. Local administrators have estimated that the
homesteading process requires approximately 100 total hours
of staff for each successfully rehabilitated property.[18]

Program staff interact with selected homeowners on an
individual basis to plan the rehabilitation work, to arrange
financing, and to monitor the terms of agreements. A
variety of skills are required. Underestimation of staffing
requirements was not uncommon among homesteading
demonstration cities. The number of program staff ranged
from one to eleven full-time equivalents (with an average of
eight) by the third year.[19] In most cases this expansion
signaled program maturity and experience rather than program
growth. Varying commitments of staff time are also directly
related to the scope and design of each program--especially
as related to control over property rehabilitation.

Guidelines

The broad guidelines established by Congress in the
Housing and Community Development Act of 1974 aimed to
ensure the fairness, timely completion, and coordination of
urban homesteading with other neighborhood improvement
efforts--not to dictate specific procedures for satisfying
these requirements.[20] The requirement of a coordinated
approach toward neighborhood improvement prohibited either
scattered site or citywide homesteading. Local governments
were thus to specify their own goals and design programs
based upon local considerations within this framework.

Section 810 legislation imposes three important
milestones upon the local urban homesteading process.
First, in the initial (1974) guidelines, the homesteader was

allowed eighteen months to   make repairs,   meeting minimal
health and safety standards for occupancy after conditional
conveyance of the property.   Second, within three years of
the date of occupancy, the homesteader was to   complete
rehabilitation work   conforming to   local building-code
standards.   Third,   to   encourage   individual   family
homeownership and discourage speculation,   the legislation
required   homesteaders to   remain   occupants of   their
properties for at least three years.   One other program
change resulted from public opinion: program beneficiaries
and displacement.   Localities are now directed to give
priority to families paying more than 30 percent of their
income for shelter,   currently residing in substandard
structures,   and who have little prospect for improved
conditions.   In addition, the homesteader must now occupy
the property as a principal residence for five--instead of
three--years and bring it up to code within three years--
instead of   eighteen   months--after   occupancy.   The
opportunity for "sweat equity"--theoretically a boon to
lower-income households--is maximized under these extended
time lines.   HUD headquarters also   provides program
procedures for area managers for the listing of HUD-owned
properties, establishing fair market values, transferring
properties for use in approved urban homesteading programs,
and reimbursing the HUD-FHA insurance fund, the VA, and the
Department of Agriculture.
    In 1979 Section 810 program criteria underwent some
important changes.   Congress sought to expand the inventory
of   federal   properties   suitable   for homesteading   by
authorizing reimbursement   for   available   VA and   FmHA
foreclosed properties to the Veterans Administration and the
Department of Agriculture, respectively.   In fiscal year
1982 VA properties became eligible under Section 810 for the
first time. This change reflects the significant decline in
the overall HUD-owned housing inventory, which had reached
its peak in the mid-1970s with the continued interest in
urban homesteading.
    The inventory   of HUD-owned vacant   properties had
declined from over 75,000 properties at the end of 1974 to
17,238 properties as of September 30, 1982.   But the
transfer of HUD properties to local urban homesteading
programs under Section 810 accounted for only 2.5 percent of
all HUD-owned properties disposed of since 1975.   A higher
percentage might have been observed in some individual
homesteading communities and cities. The number of incoming
properties available for urban homesteading each year is
potentially substantial.   During 1982, HUD acquired 18,179
properties, compared to 13,871 in 1981.   The overall
inventory, however, still declined because sales exceeded
acquisitions.
    HUD's direct support of additional property sources for
homesteading can be considered an acknowledgment that a
larger pool of houses must be improved if this small program
is to have an impact in a community. In 1984, city-acquired
properties became eligible for purchase using Section 810
funds, and a multi-family urban homesteading demonstration
program is in the early operational stages in some cities.

Local Discretion: Property and Homesteader Selection

Strategies for property selection and homesteader selection are interrelated policy issues.   Both infer local goals and affect the outcome of the homesteading effort.[21] Participating cities determine the number, size, and location of the homesteading properties chosen from HUD's inventory.   The rehabilitated values of properties relative to the 810 values of the properties will have ramifications for possible program participants.   The issues are not easy to delineate, but main points have been extracted from the experiences of demonstration and operating cities.   Two major approaches to property selection have been observed, the first involving the selection of properties with higher 810 values and low rehabilitation costs.   The financial burden for homesteaders and technical demands on agency staff are commensurately reduced, but the number of properties that can be homesteaded is limited.   The alternative is to select properties with lower 810 values, which may enable the use of more structures but increases rehabilitation costs, financing needs, and agency costs. The condition of available properties, the amount of financing available, and other program objectives influence the effects of either approach.

During the early stages of the program, administrators experienced a learning period.   Some, saddled with badly deteriorated or otherwise unattractive properties, changed selection criteria to take into account structural features requested by homesteaders or the condition of the surrounding neighborhood.   Cities either relaxed or tightened standards in property selection.   Those anxious to maintain an urban homesteading program relaxed criteria when faced with a declining HUD inventory and rejected few, if any, properties.   Similarly, some cities enlarged their neighborhood boundaries to deal with increased HUD offerings.[22]

Homesteader selection comprises three major subtasks: program publicity and marketing; applicant evaluation and screening; and matching homeowners with properties.   Program publicity and marketing is generally acknowledged as the least demanding responsibility.   The method or content of outreach consistently yielded a high volume of response; however, the more specific the announcements and information, the greater the proportion of qualified applicants.

Processing and screening applicants, the most time-consuming phase, may differ in participants and procedure. Participants can involve a combination of staff, broad-based review boards and/or community groups.   Procedures, required by the program legislation to be fair and equitable, include a mixture of judgmental screening (by review boards) and objective screening (assessment of ability to secure financing).   Some objective criteria could become subjective in effect, such as ability to secure private financing. Clearly, level of income is directly related to one's likelihood in meeting this criterion.   Lotteries have also been employed in the selection process at different points for different purposes. They have been used to reduce the number of initial applicants, to designate potential homesteaders from applicants deemed eligible, and to determine the order in which homesteaders will choose properties.

Matching homesteaders with properties may occur at different points in the process but is the penultimate consideration. The action may result from a lottery, homesteader choice, or board action. Although the urban homesteading authorizing legislation (prior to 1984) specified only that cities consider the applicant's need for housing and his/her capacity to make or cause to be made repairs to the property, all the demonstration cities used additional eligibility factors. These can be categorized as follows:

. Demographic criteria;
. Previous housing tenure/housing need;
. Financial criteria;
. Self-help skills;
. Social behavior and attitude.

Such criteria can be modified to enhance programmatic goals and objectives. And in a similar fashion, goals can influence property selection.

By selecting properties that require less rehabilitation, the amount of financing--public and/or private--that the homesteader must arrange is reduced. Properties with higher rehabilitation values require homesteaders with greater financial or technical capacity. Cities must decide who has the ability to secure the necessary financing, given the resources available. During the demonstration, it was found that homesteaders who undertake substantial rehabilitation tend to rely more heavily on government loan programs. This increases the amount of financing required and the administrative burden of arranging it.

The location of the property and condition of the surrounding neighborhood affect any decision to purchase a home. The demonstration evaluation found that in sixteen out of twenty-three cases, a goal of attracting new residents to homesteading neighborhoods was implied because no preference was given to existing residents in selecting homesteaders.[23]

Property selection can directly affect homesteader eligibility as related to program goals. If local officials wish to create homeownership opportunities for families who could not compete in the local housing market, they must select properties within their means. Program managers are better able to assess this situation if the target population is reliant upon public funds for rehabilitation financing, e.g., Section 312 loans.

The demonstration cities' study included information comparing homesteaders to their neighbors in the target areas. Selected demographic and socioeconomic

characteristics of homesteaders were compared with those of
all residents (who were broken down by tenure type) and with
residents who have lived in the homesteading neighborhoods
for less than two years ("movers-in").   Homesteaders were
quite similar to all other residents in terms of race.   More
significantly, homesteaders were younger and more affluent
than the average owner in their neighborhoods.

Incomes of urban homesteaders also shed some light on
the issue of gentrification.   In 1979,   the average
homesteader nationally had an income of $17,000, slightly
below the national average of $17,730.   The mean income of
Philadelphia homesteaders in 1979 was $20,450; the overall
city mean was $21,192.   For the same period, the mean
homesteader income in Baltimore was $14,897; the city mean,
$16,187.   In Philadelphia and Baltimore, all homesteaders
included in the demonstration--sixty-seven and thirteen,
respectively--were black.   Clearly, at least in its early
stages, urban homesteading did not appear to encourage
gentrification or displacement.

Local Discretion: Financing and Managing Rehabilitation

The urban homesteader may be faced with inherent
problems of securing financing in areas suffering from
disinvestment. Program support that governments can attract
from the private sector can enhance the program by leveraging public dollars.   Most, if not all, urban homesteading
programs offer a variety of means for financing homestead
rehabilitation.   Each of the first twenty-three
demonstration cities offered at least one of the three
general types of city-assisted financing: city-assisted
loans through banks and savings and loan associations,
municipal or county loan programs, and Section 312 loans.
Sixty-seven percent of all homesteaders who started work
under this program utilized city-assisted loan financing for
at least a portion of the rehabilitation.[24]   The main
obstacle in arranging for direct private lending to
homesteaders is that the loan request does not qualify as a
standard home improvement or home mortgage loan.
Homesteaders do not hold clear title to their properties
initially and have little or no cash equity at the outset.
Eleven demonstration cities successfully resolved these
issues and secured private financing--either for
homesteading specifically or in conjunction with other
existing rehabilitation programs that served the broader
population.   Other supplemental assistance includes tax
exemptions or abatements and outright grants, tools that are
especially tied into policy considerations and local fiscal
conditions.   Demonstration project homesteaders usually
secured financing.   Although the practice of "creaming"
(that is, selection of those most likely to qualify)
undoubtedly occurred, only five homesteaders dropped out
because they were unable to obtain financing.[25]

The fundamental issue in rehabilitation management is
control.   The degree of involvement of the homesteading

agency   staff--specifying   and   assigning   repairs   and
monitoring the work--reflects program   goals and the overall
rehabilitation   approach.   The   demonstration   cities'
evaluation identified   three groups   of cities   with similar
rehabilitation   strategies.   One   group   of   five   cities
emphasized high quality-control standards,   rapid completion
of repairs,   and a high degree   of agency control   over the
specification and performance of work.   Homesteaders' input
was minimized throughout the process although eventually all
but one city modified self-help policies.
     A   second   group   of   thirteen   cities   maintained   less
stringent   rehabilitation   standards   and emphasized   greater
homesteader   participation   in   work   planning,   contractor
selection, and a controlled use of sweat equity (repair work
completed by   the homesteader).   Philadelphia was   one such
city.   In the third group,   five cities had less stringent
standards   of   rehabilitation,   encouraged   significant
homesteader involvement in work   planning,   generally placed
more reliance on homesteaders for contractor selection,   and
encouraged the use of sweat equity.   Baltimore was in this
group.   Recall that Detroit was not a demonstration city and
was not included in the evaluation.
     Inferences   about   the   cities'   urban   homesteading
objectives   can   be   based   upon   their   approaches   to
rehabilitation.   Cities   in the   first two   groups seem   to
place   higher   priority   on   quality   and   speed   of
rehabilitation;   the third group   appeared more   concerned
about cost   control and fostering homesteader   attachment to
the property.   The anticipated trade-off of cost for quality
in "sweat equity"   did not manifest itself.   Management of
the local program,   rather than the   agent of repair,   was a
more important determinant of   the quality of workmanship.[26]
A study conducted for the   President's Commission on Housing
found that,   overall, where self-help completed a substantial
portion of   the work,   rehabilitation generally   took longer
but   produced   work   that   was   equal   in   quality   to   that
performed   by   professional   contractors.[27]   The   report
concluded   that   sweat   equity   is   compatible   with   quality
repairs and cost reduction.
     Under the operating program,   some communities use sweat
equity   to   allow   homesteader   contributions   to   the
rehabilitation of their homesteads.   In   its 1983 Report to
Congress on Community Development   Programs,   HUD found that
self-help is generally encouraged,   but   has been limited by
local rules   (that require homesteaders   to be   certified or
licensed prior to undertaking technical work such as wiring,
plumbing, and heating) and by local provisions that restrict
sweat-equity   contributions   to   cosmetic   property
improvements.
     During the demonstration, all local governments provided
full or   partial property tax relief   during the   residency
period.   This was not as commonly the case in the operating
program,   as few units of   government seemed willing or able
to forgo tax revenue and incur the loss in income.   As part
of   the HUD   inventory,   property taxes   were   paid by   the
federal government.

FINDINGS OF DEMONSTRATION PROGRAM EVALUATION

The most comprehensive assessment of the Urban Homesteading Program focuses upon the four years of the demonstration, which began in Fall 1975. The original enabling legislation had mandated an evaluation at the end of the demonstration period. Generally positive conclusions about various facets of the program were drawn; future prospects for program development and expansion were deemed promising. Some of the pertinent, major conclusions enumerated were:

1. The participating cities designed efficient, manageable homesteading organizations and successfully resolved minor administrative difficulties. A wide variation in administrative arrangements resulted from the flexible HUD guidelines. CDBG was the primary source of funds for operating expenses.

2. Although cities exercised wide latitude in their approaches toward the planning and management of rehabilitation, repairs generally occurred in a timely fashion and to high standards. Compared to cities that offered greater latitude to the homesteader, cities that exercised a high degree of control over the process completed rehabilitation more quickly, but no apparent difference in quality of workmanship and choice of materials resulted.

3. The socioeconomic decline of urban homesteading neighborhoods was arrested or considerably moderated during the period of the demonstration. The evaluation found that relative decline in the income of neighborhood residents was arrested; and changes in the median income of neighborhood residents approximated the national experience. Racial change, which had characterized the earlier period, continued: but at a slower pace. In addition, the evaluation found little evidence of displacement in these neighborhoods. Between 1977 and 1979, a significant increase in investment activity by owner-occupants occurred in terms of frequency of investing and the average investment expenditures. In the latter case, the increase in owner-occupant investment exceeded the national average. Property values, which had declined relative to those in the rest of the SMSAs (Standard Metropolitan Statistical Areas), maintained their relative position during the Demonstration. The Urban Homesteading neighborhoods were no longer losing ground

after 1977 when compared with control neighborhoods in the same cities.

4. The rehabilitation and reoccupancy of homestead properties appears to have had a direct, positive influence on the immediately surrounding properties and an overall impact on the stabilization of the homestead neighborhoods. There is no proof that improvements in the neighborhoods directly resulted from urban homesteading activities, particularly since homesteading properties accounted for less than 2 percent of the dwelling units in such areas. In general, however, the demonstration's neighborhood stabilization objective was fulfilled, and there is substantial evidence that urban homesteading contributed to that accomplishment.

Findings of the GAO Report

Although critical of HUD's administration of the Urban Homesteading Program in early years, a 1979 GAO report concluded that it had exerted a positive influence on nearly every neighborhood observed. Results, however, were uneven in terms of the time required to homestead houses and containment of rehabilitation costs.[28]

GAO also noticed an escalation in the values and the general condition of the houses acquired by HUD as the program matured. This probably reflects adverse local experiences with lower quality properties. The report cautioned against including high-value houses because this would be a significant departure from the original programs (in Baltimore, Philadelphia, and Wilmington) where basically sound, but unmarketable, houses were used. Further, they indicated that in neighborhoods showing few signs of blight and where houses are marketable, giving away high-value HUD houses is unnecessary. This was particularly observed in the cities of Tacoma and Dallas.[29]

Two other observations are noteworthy: pertaining to the relationship of HUD area office staff and Urban Homesteading Program staff. First, GAO concluded that homesteading programs appeared to be more effective where a close relationship existed between HUD and participating communities. In those situations, each house had a clear disposition plan established, and it was carried out in a timely manner. Secondly, HUD was criticized for not adequately monitoring the demonstration program to improve administration and take corrective action as needed. In the case studies of Baltimore and Philadelphia, monitoring proved to be a major variable in urban homesteading implementation.

Although HUD expressed some disagreement with the GAO report, it did implement some of the recommendations. These

included (1) identifying successful homesteading methods and
making recommendations for program design; (2) developing
monitoring and reporting systems; (3) terminating a program
(Tacoma, Washington) where it was no longer needed; and (4)
the use of the monitoring system to detect other programs
appropriate for termination.

In a letter of commitment, however, HUD Assistant
Secretary Robert C. Embry, Jr., rejected any modification
that would infringe upon the flexibility needed "to keep the
urban homesteading concept alive and responsive to local
needs."

DEVELOPMENTS IN THE FEDERAL PROGRAM

The revised Section 810 legislation enacted in 1984 is
consistent with the views of HUD area office representatives
in Baltimore and Philadelphia who asserted that federal
programs inevitably gravitate toward more restrictions.
From the time it assumed operating status in 1978 to 1984,
however, the regulations governing the urban homesteading
program remained virtually untouched. The Housing and
Urban-Rural Recovery Act of 1983 legislated the most
significant program changes, nudging participating
localities in a direction that would benefit lower-income
persons. The act also provided funds to facilitate greater
use of the homesteading concept, with particular emphasis
upon lower-income families. The 1983 Act:

1.   For the first time, imposed a requirement
     regarding homesteader selection procedures so
     as to target benefits. Localities must now
     give special priority to applicants whose
     current housing is substandard (fails to meet
     health and safety standards), who pay more
     than 30 percent of their income for shelter,
     and who have little likelihood of obtaining
     improved housing without homesteading.
     Current homeowners are prohibited from
     participating as homesteaders.

2.   Changes that would allow more time for the use
     of sweat equity. The deadline for completion
     of rehabilitation work was increased from
     eighteen months to three years and the
     required occupancy period was increased from
     three years to five years.

3.   Provided additional stimulus for sweat equity
     by requiring that localities give positive
     consideration in the selection process to an
     applicant's capacity to do substantial
     rehabilitation himself/herself and the
     applicant's ability to secure other materials
     and financing from private sources, community
     organizations, or other sources.

4. Established a multi-family homesteading demonstration program using HUD-owned multi-family properties during 1984 and 1985. Seventy-five percent of the occupants must be lower-income families.

5. Authorized $1 million annually in 1984 and 1985 for a demonstration program to test the feasibility of providing assistance to state and local governments for the purchase of one-to four-family properties to be conveyed to lower-income families.

The 1983 Act also requires a statement of local goals for each homesteading neighborhood. Such a statement enables both HUD and the applicant to more easily judge whether the program is achieving the intended results and whether the applicant's procedures are conducive to meeting local goals. Significantly, the regulations give HUD new authority to waive legally mandated regulatory provisions when undue hardship to applying localities would result or the requirement would adversely affect the achievement of program purposes. With this "regulated deregulation," cities can deviate from the regulations with HUD's approval. The ambivalence of public policymaking is observed in the enactment of stricter requirements with a provision to bypass them in the same legislation.

It is probable that community activists had some influence on the 1983 changes. In June 1982, Congress held hearings on urban homesteading. The hearings included testimony of low-income housing advocates from major cities who were critical of locally run efforts. Many of the speakers had begun illegal squatting in vacant homes. Most testimony lamented the inability of lower-income persons to participate in the program due to financing problems. Urban Homesteading is unusual among current housing programs because it does not fall under the CDBG umbrella; it is, therefore, more directly subject to federal legislative influence. The possibility of federal government intervention gave these activists another audience for their grievances besides local officials.

CONCLUSION

This research began with the assumption that significant differences would be observed in the way cities structured the administration of their Urban Homesteading Programs. This chapter indicated that the amount of deviation among administrative components is restricted by several factors. First, the federal guidelines set forth a stringent context in which localities must conduct urban homesteading: programs must operate in specifically targeted neighborhoods and with a coordinated approach. In addition, funds for administration and rehabilitation must come from other sources. Faced with such conditions, the subject cities did

not have much room to maneuver. CDBG funds were
overwhelmingly used to operate the program; a minimal number
of neighborhoods, properties, and individuals could be
helped. The more significant issues become: How did cities
make decisions related to program beneficiaries? And how did
these decisions impact program outcomes? Contrary to the
five-volume evaluation of the urban homesteading
demonstration, significant differences in approaches did
impact operating program outcomes.

The necessary components of the Urban Homesteading
Program (as illustrated in Figure 1) comprise a second
factor that inhibits deviation in administrative approaches.
These elements are defined in the legislation, and the
requisite steps involved are fairly straightforward. The
possible variation in the sequencing and overlap of
activities do not appear to be significant determinants of
program outcomes. The goals and objectives pursued by each
city are the most significant variables. Procedural components function to support them.

Urban homesteading legislation has experienced few
significant changes related to program focus. Additional
properties are now eligible for homesteading; lower-income
households must now be given priority. These changes
moderate the discretionary aspect of the program.
Conversely, there have been no changes in direct support of
the program, that is, for administration and rehabilitation.
The regulations, in essence, have become more imposing with
no additional incentives to offset negative reactions from
localities.

Having examined the common programmatic and
administrative variables that affect urban homesteading
implementation and having observed how cities can vary
within the program guidelines, we will take a closer look at
three settings for implementation: Baltimore, Detroit, and
Philadelphia.

NOTES

1. HUD, Evaluation of the Urban Homesteading
Demonstration Program: Final Report. 5 vols. (Washington,
D.C.: GPO, 1981), vol. 2, p. 10.
    2. Ibid., p. 9.
    3. Ibid., p. 1.
    4. Ibid., p. 3.
    5. Ibid., p. 4.
    6. Ibid., p. 151.
    7. HUD, The Urban Homesteading Catalog, 1977,
(Washington, D.C.: GPO), vol. 3, p. 3.
    8. Ibid., p. 5.
    9. HUD, Evaluation of the Urban Homesteading Program,
(Washington, D.C.: GPO), vol. 2, p. 13.
    10. Ibid., p. 19.
    11. GAO, Report to the Congress of the United States.
Urban Homesteading, 1979, p. 56.
    12. The 810 value is defined as the fair market value
minus the estimated carrying cost that HUD would incur to

hold the properties for conventional disposition.

13. HUD, _Evaluation of the Urban Homesteading Demonstration Program_, vol. 2, p. 31.

14. Ibid., p. 32.

15. Ibid., p. 29.

16. Ibid., p. 30.

17. Ibid., p. 35.

18. Ibid., p. 32.

19. Ibid., p. 32.

20. Ibid., p. 28.

21. Ibid., p. 41.

22. Ibid., p. 43.

23. Ibid., p. 47.

24. Ibid., p. 58.

25. Ibid., p. 68.   _Evaluation of the Urban Homesteading Demonstration Program_,

26. Ibid., p. 78

27. Howard Sumka, "Urban Homesteading", Report prepared for HUD, 1981, p. 6.

28. GAO, _Urban Homesteading_, 1979, p. 35.

29. Ibid., p. 36.

5

Three Settings for Section 810 Implementation

The choice of Baltimore, Detroit, and Philadelphia as subjects provides an opportunity to compare three different patterns of urban homesteading implementation. The program began in Baltimore as the product of local initiative; establishment of the federal Section 810 Urban Homesteading program occurred later. Philadelphia also developed a local program prior to the enactment of the federal version. Both cities were early participants in the first round of Section 810 Urban Homesteading Demonstration Cities. Detroit entered the urban homesteading arena later, beginning with the Section 810 operating program and establishing a local program much later.

Similarities as well as differences exist among the subject cities. Similarities include mayor-council governance, overall population losses after 1950, losses in occupied housing units after 1960, sizable black populations (over 25 percent since 1960), and growing proportions of low-income persons. (See Tables 5.1, 5.2, and 5.3). Significant differences include political party structures and influence, and community development settings. These characteristics--and their bearing upon the implementation of urban homesteading--are presented in this chapter.

AN OVERVIEW

Michael C. D. Macdonald has found that the fiscal futures of all major urban cities have been impacted by federal cuts: losses in CETA jobs; cuts in health services, social services, and school lunch programs; support for welfare and food stamps; and other forms of support. In America's Cities: A Report on the Myth of Urban Renaissance, he classified Baltimore, Detroit, and Philadelphia as among the nation's five "disaster cities."[1] Ironically, Macdonald's book was released the same day as Esquire Magazine's profile naming Baltimore's former mayor, William Donald Schaefer, the best mayor in America.[2] According to A Housing Strategy for the City of Detroit, by Ray Struyk and David Rasmussen,[3] Detroit and Philadelphia

TABLE 5.1
POPULATION DATA

CATEGORY	BALTIMORE			DETROIT			PHILADELPHIA		
	Total	Change	Percent	Total	Change	Percent	Total	Change	Percent
Population									
1980	787,775	-117,984	-13.0	1,203,339	308,143	-20.4	1,688,210	-260,399	-13.4
1970	905,759	-33,265	-3.5	1,511,482	-158,662	-9.5	1,948,609	-53,903	-2.7
1960	939,024	-10,684	-1.1	1,670,144	-179,426	-9.7	2,002,512	-69,093	-3.3
1950	949,708	90,608	10.5	1,849,568	226,116	13.9	2,071,605	140,271	7.3
1940	859,100	54,226	6.7	1,623,452	54,790	3.5	1,931,334	-19,627	-1.0
1930	804,874	71,048	9.7	1,568,662	574,984	57.4	1,950,961	127,182	7.0
1920	733,826	175,341	31.4	993,678	527,912	113.3	1,823,779	274,771	17.0
1910	558,486	49,528	9.7	465,766	180,062	63.0	1,549,008	255,311	19.7
1900	508,957			285,704			1,293,697		

TABLE 5.2 DEMOGRAPHIC DATA			
CATEGORY	BALTIMORE	DETROIT	PHILADELPHIA
% Blacks and Other Minorities			
1980	56	65	41
1970	47	44.5	34.4
1960	35	29.2	26.7
Median Income			
1980	$12,811	$13,981	$13,169
1970	8,815	10,145	9,366
1960	6,196	6,825	6,433
% Below Poverty Level			
1980	22.9	21.9	20.6
1970	14.0	11.3	11.2
% Below $3,000 in 1960	14.3	13.5	13.0

are classified as severely declining cities in declining Standard Metropolitan Statistical Areas (SMSAs). Baltimore, Philadelphia, and Detroit are similar in per capita income and in the importance of manufacturing development.

A Princeton University study compared American cities according to an index based upon housing age, per capita income, and population change between 1960 and 1977. Examining social and economic conditions in the nation's ninety-seven largest cities, the report showed that the country's older urban areas are becoming poorer and less populated despite renewal efforts. The report grouped cities into five categories, from most distressed to least distressed. Detroit and Philadelphia were among the most distressed, while Baltimore was classified as slightly less distressed.

Clearly, the subject cities have shared some problems. The blight of neighborhood deterioration contributed to the introduction of urban homesteading as a possible solution. Each city discussed here used urban homesteading differently to pursue varying objectives. The discretion inherent in the Urban Homesteading Program makes it adaptable to ostensibly different ends. The local environments in the three cities are discussed to assess how they shaped the programs' operations.

CATEGORY	BALTIMORE	DETROIT	PHILADELPHIA
TABLE 5.3 HOUSING DATA			

CATEGORY	BALTIMORE	DETROIT	PHILADELPHIA
Total Year Round Housing Units			
1980	302,459	471,155	685,271
1970	305,464	529,043	673,390
1960	290,155	553,198	648,942
Total Occupied Housing Units			
1980	281,414	433,488	619,781
1970	289,349	497,755	642,145
1960	275,597	514,846	615,699
Vacancy Rate (Homeowners)			
1980	1.3	1.3	1.8
1970	0.9	1.5	1.0
Vacancy Rate (Rental)			
1980	5.4	9.4	7.5
1970	5.8	9.2	5.6
Owner Occupied (Total Percent)			
1980	132,735/47.2	250,887/57.8	378,129/61.0
1970	128,730/44.5	298,624/60.0	383,630/59.7
1960	149,684/54.3	299,507/58.2	381,171/61.9
Renter Occupied (Total/Percent)			
1980	148,679/52.8	182,601/42.1	241,652/39.0
1970	160,586/55.5	199,219/40.0	258,515/40.3
1960	125,913/45.7	215,339/41.8	234,528/38.1
Median Housing Value			
1980	$28,900	$21,000	$23,700
1970	10,300	15,600	10,600
1960	6,200	12,800	9,400
Median Contract Rent			
1980	$161	$154	$168
1970	88	80	76
1960	70	67	62
Year Built (%)			
1970-March, 1980	5.8	3.2	5.5
1939 or earlier	50.3	45.6	58.4

BALTIMORE

General Description

The largest city in Maryland, Baltimore encompasses an area of ninety-two square miles. Sizable losses of population and industry have had significant impact upon Baltimore's housing situation and on its ability to generate own-source revenues. The city's population declined 3.5 percent between 1960 and 1970: from 939,024 to 905,759 (1960 and 1970 censuses); a more drastic decrease of 13 percent occurred between 1970 and 1980, down to 787,775.

Two recent trends have surfaced within this twenty-year time frame. The black population, as a percentage of the total population, has grown significantly. In 1960, blacks comprised 35 percent of the population; in 1970, 47 percent; and in 1980, 56 percent. While the median income in Baltimore increased from 1960 to 1980, in the latter year nearly 23 percent of the population fell below the poverty level. (See Table 5.2.) The situation in Baltimore reflects population changes that are common to older, urban, industrialized areas.

From an economic standpoint, Baltimore has been billed as the largest "unknown" city in the world. It is conservative, blue collar, and industrial. According to Fortune's industrial ratings, only one of the country's top 500 companies has its headquarters there--Crown Petroleum. The less favorable aspects of Baltimore have been partially contradicted by the planners, architects, urban administrators, and housing officials who have named it one of the nation's most livable cities.[4]

Baltimore is more functionally self-contained than the majority of cities in the United States.[5] The city does not lie within the boundaries of any county but operates as a freestanding subdivision directly subordinate to the state of Maryland--with the same powers as counties. As a result, functions such as welfare and waste disposal--in addition to public schools--are administered by the city government. While this arrangement allows for considerable autonomy, the city must assume the costs of providing these services.

Baltimore is a city of neighborhoods. This trait has historic and geographic foundations. For years, the city was a point of entry for immigrants who settled strong ethnic neighborhoods. In addition, both the city's naturally hilly terrain and its man-made divisions, such as roads and railroads, have helped to create a variety of distinctive areas. There are some 300 coherently established and identifiable neighborhoods and about 100 active neighborhood organizations in Baltimore.[6]

Once a place where immigrants could improve their skills, increase their income, and find new and better housing, Baltimore is no longer accomplishing its traditional task of providing economic and social opportunity for newcomers.[7] Since 1960, most new housing and industry have been established outside its boundaries.

Particularly in comparison with its suburban neighbors, the
city became poorer and more segregated as its tax base
weakened.

Local Political Culture

The current structure of Baltimore city government is
highly centralized. In 1898, during the era of reform and
good government movements, a major charter reform greatly
increased mayoral power. That power depends upon three
major factors: control of the appointment of department
heads (a personal merit system exists below that rank);
control over the fiscal and budgetary processes through the
Departments of Finance and Board of Estimates; and the
ability to veto city council ordinances.[8] The mayor appoints
three members of the five-person Board of Estimates,
established to oversee the city's fiscal policies. The Board
of Finance, consisting of the mayor, the comptroller, and
three other mayoral appointees, manages municipal debt. The
mayor presides over the board.
In 1922, the Baltimore city council switched from a
bicameral to a unicameral legislative body. The council
consists of nineteen members, three of whom are elected from
each of six districts and the president, who is elected at-
large. Formally, the council's work includes the review of
ordinances and resolutions as well as the mayor's
legislative package. A three-fourths council majority can
override a mayoral veto or call for a suspension of the
rules; however, this rarely occurs. City council members
have, furthermore, become dependent upon the mayor for any
patronage and extraordinary service to constituents. This
dependency has become an even more critical problem as the
fiscal stress of the 1970s has greatly constrained available
resources.[9]
William Donald Schaefer, Democratic mayor of Baltimore
from 1971 to 1987, was the latest in a succession of strong
mayors. The local and federal urban homesteading programs
were operated during his tenure as chief elected official.
At the time of his election, Baltimore suffered from low
morale and a century-old inferiority complex. The city's
depiction as a corridor between New York and Washington,
D.C., denigrated its status. Schaefer's agenda gave priority
to neighborhood restoration, reversal of white middle class
flight to the suburbs, and strengthening the city's pride
and identity.[10]
It was difficult to find political opposition to
Schaefer. Even blacks, who would have preferred a black
mayor were quick to mention that Schaefer was a good mayor
who does not play racial politics. His only consistent
critic was former council chairman Walter Orlinsky, who
attacked Shaefer for creating an image that made any attack
on him an attack on Baltimore.[11]
Schaefer was challenged when running for his fourth term
in 1983, by Democrat William H. Murphy, Jr. Murphy's was the
first serious challenge by a black candidate for the

Baltimore mayoralty. His campaign focused upon housing and
education that had been sacrificed for the bricks and mortar
of downtown development. He lost handily in the primary, and
Schaefer went on to easily defeat his Republican challenger
in the general election. That same year, the city elected
its first black council president, Clarence DuBurns.

Schaefer was victorious in Maryland's 1987 gubernatorial
election. His movement out of local politics paved the way
for the election of the city's first black mayor. In a run-
off election Clarence DuBurns was defeated by Kurt Schmoke.

Matthew Crenson identifies a three-part amalgam in
Baltimore which constitutes an executive-centered coalition.
(This pattern of mayoral influence and policymaking was
first identified in Robert Dahl's study of New Haven and
later elaborated upon by Robert Salisbury.[12] State and
federal grants that constituted more than half of the city's
annual budget is one ingredient.   Schaefer is largely
credited with winning this support, especially from
Washington. A second ingredient is the unwavering support of
the local business community, organized into the Greater
Baltimore Committee for the purpose of civic action. Third
is the compliance of the city's bureaucratic agencies, which
bent to Schaefer's will and temper during his years in
office. The pattern became fully developed during downtown
urban renewal efforts in the late 1970s.

Mayor Schaefer's influence was aided by fragmentation in
the community, which contrasted with his centralized
government. Party politics are weak in Baltimore. The role
and strength of organized political activity have been
eroded by a tradition of neighborhood influence and a loss
of power formerly exercised through patronage positions. As
a city of neighborhoods, Baltimore is characterized by ward
politics and political machines. Levine has noted that the
Democratic clubs have lost some influence due to population
changes that have altered neighborhoods. He comments that
the Democratic label in Baltimore demonstrates little about
shared views; again, the city's distinctive neighborhood
history in particular and Maryland politics in general
contribute to this variety.[13] Mayor Schaefer's formal
authority was enhanced by this as well as the part-time
status of at least half of the city council members.

The role of citizen participation is almost axiomatic in
Baltimore. Umbrella neighborhood organizations created since
1968 have partially upstaged council members in providing
services to citizens. These organizations receive financial
support from CDBG funds. A number of these groups house
local branches of the mayor's office, which promote direct
linkages to City Hall.

A survey of twenty-two cities conducted by the council
on Municipal Performance reported that Baltimore was most
responsive to its citizens. The council credited four types
of "citizen communication channels"--an ombudsman, a mayor's
community affairs aide, complaint lines (direct lines for
citizen complaints to agencies), and a system of
neighborhood government offices.   Further, Baltimore's
committee meetings were reported "routinely open to the

public" and "activists are included in the planning of
economic development. . . ."[14]

A highway system proposed to traverse the city center
aroused fierce protest during the 1960s and 1970s. Even
though the government was to pay 90 percent of the
construction cost, local officials objected on the grounds
that it represented bad planning. During the early 1970s,
when citizen groups coalesced as Movement Against
Destruction (MAD), the press and influential residents
successfully protested a city council decision that would
have permitted construction of the interstate highway
directly through the Inner Harbor. The alternative plan--
which was adopted--allowed traffic to go in and out of the
central business district, but not to pass directly through
it.[15]

Fiscal Setting

Economic-base erosion and increased dependence on
intergovernmental aid are the most salient characteristics
of Baltimore's recent fiscal history.[16] As financial
dependence upon state and federal dollars has increased, the
city's population has decreased, the assessable property tax
base has shown little or no growth, and the cost of
providing public services has increased. City officials have
employed many administrative tactics in an attempt to
maintain a balance between expenditures and revenues.
Attention and resources have been divided between
maintaining city services and revitalization efforts.

Baltimore's revitalization activities are attenuated by
simultaneous fiscal stress. A comparison of Baltimore with
the surrounding area emphasizes its relative deprivation.
The Baltimore region has maintained economic significance in
the state while the city's stability has been eroded. The
discrepancy between Baltimore and the suburbs is apparent in
a number of areas. Population in the surrounding area has
continued to grow while Baltimore's population has declined.
Those remaining in the central city are comparatively poorer
and more service dependent. In 1960, the median Baltimore
income was 78.5 percent of that in the suburbs. By 1978 it
had declined to 62.4 percent.

From the beginning of his first term, Schaefer made
fiscal responsibility a priority. Municipal employment
dropped from 38,000 to 35,000 after he ordered a freeze on
hiring in 1972. A tough conservation plan consisting of
sharp cutbacks in fuel and other supplies saved the city $10
million over the last two years of his first term. The
city maintained a bare-bones budget under Schaefer, which
resulted in a boost in the city's credit rating from "A" to
"A-1" in 1975.

Despite these efforts, Baltimore has been unable to
generate sufficient own-source revenues to counteract the
effects of demographic changes. Only a slight increase in
the assessable tax base occurred duing the 1970s. That
increase can be attributed to: (1) an increase in the

proportion of tax-exempt (largely city-owned) property, and
(2) state-minded changes that resulted in a decrease in the
assessable base in both 1975 and 1979. Given the inadequate
growth of own-source revenues, economic-base erosion, and
the level of services provided, state and federal aid has
played an increasingly important role in keeping Baltimore
solvent.

During the 1970s, Baltimore successfully secured a large
amount of state aid, benefiting from its status as a city-
county and from powerful legislative and lobbying
delegations. The state has traditionally dispensed large
amounts of aid at the county level.   State and federal aid
constituted 54.8 percent of the operating budget in 1973;
58.5 percent in 1979; 62 percent in 1980; and 58 percent in
fiscal 1982-83.   State funds comprised an unprecedented 85
percent of the intergovernmental revenue received by the
city in 1982-83.   The city finished fiscal 1975 with a $52
million surplus because the state had relieved it of all
fiscal responsibility for mass transit, school construction,
assessment of property for tax purposes, and the nonfederal
share of welfare costs.   The state is also paying a major
portion of the city's health services and police protection
costs.   [17]

State legislative support is noteworthy. Maryland State
Senator Victor Crawford was quoted as saying that "Baltimore
is very important to Maryland. . . .   It's obvious to us in
the Senate that Baltimore is trying, and that the problems
they have aren't due to fiscal mismanagement."[18] In spite of
the deepening reliance upon the considerable provision of
intergovernmental aid, such aid has not totally filled the
city's revenue-expenditure gap.

Several major public employee unions represent
Baltimore's municipal employees. The city's limited ability
to meet the economic demands of public employees has been
the focal point of labor-management problems.   The unions
have experienced marginal success in winning benefits and
wage increases for members. Levine contrasts the role of
unions in Baltimore--a by-product of fiscal problems--with
the role of New York City unions, which are viewed as part
of the problem. The unions are somewhat influential in city
politics, but do not have significant input into formal
decision-making processes.   The cooperation of public
employee unions has been regarded as essential to
revitalization efforts.[19]

Baltimore officials, headed by Mayor Schaefer, made
retrenchment decisions that have averted the resistance of
special interest groups.   Cuts have been made across-the-
board in a no-favorites manner.   Rather than borrow its way
out of crisis debt, service increases have been contained
with meager wage increases, deferral of increases, and work-
force reduction through attrition. In one of his many roles,
Mayor Schaefer successfully promoted revitalization as a
feasible solution to the city's problems--a solution that
everyone could participate in.   Whether the redevelopment
efforts will be successful enough to revitalize the city's
economic base in a timely manner remains to be seen.

Baltimore has gained fiscal control and support as other northeastern municipalities seem to be losing it. Baltimore's success with the federal government and private investors has given rise to a reputation for political efficacy at a time when it is rare among city governments.[20]

Housing and Community Development Setting

Redevelopment in Baltimore in the 1970s was personified in Mayor Schaefer. But a sequence of six mayors prior to Schaefer had maintained a high level of commitment to urban projects. Thomas D'Alessandro, Jr. (1947-59) was mayor at the inception of the Charles Center Project. He was followed by Mayor Phillip Goodman (1959) for a six-month term and by Mayor J. Harold Grady (1959-63). During this period, the Charles Center Project took form. Theodore Roosevelt McKeldin (1943-47 and 1963-67) initiated the Inner Harbor project, and Thomas D'Alessandro III (1967-71) assured its completion. He was also instrumental in the creation of the Department of Housing and Community Development (DHCD), as it is currently constituted, and in pushing for a variety of programs to serve the city's poor. When Schaefer became mayor in 1971 he had served on the city council for twenty years as both member and president. He had helped to establish some of the city's urban policies. One of his chief tasks upon election was to bring to completion a variety of projects already planned or under way.

Baltimore's DHCD is the centralized agency for the administration of all key housing and community development functions: renewal, CDBG, zoning, relocation, housing management (including public housing), economic development, and building, housing, and code enforcement. Baltimore was one of the first of the nation's largest cities to combine most of the functions connected with housing and community development into one agency. Strong leadership--similar to that of the city government--enabled the city centralized management to aggressively challenge its housing, neighborhood, and downtown problems during the 1970s which attracted national attention. DHCD also supervises contracts with four private, nonprofit corporations that perform management and economic development functions which might normally be assigned to municipal agencies: Housing Assistance Corporation; Charles Center and Inner Harbor Management Corporation (downtown redevelopment); Baltimore Economic Development Corporation (attracting and retaining industry); and Market Center Development Corporation (revitalizing the retail center).[21] Governed by trustees appointed by the mayor, these entities are unencumbered by local bureaucracy, civil service, the city charter, and the city council. They constitute what has come to be known as the Shadow Government of Baltimore.[22]

The renaissance of downtown Baltimore began in the Charles Center urban renewal area. A critical test of the partnership between the business community and the city leadership (a partnership that has become a pivotal element

in the city's life), the development resulted in the
construction of fifteen major structures, including
commercial office space, apartment units, retail commercial
uses, and a hotel.

Inner Harbor, another renewal area, occupies 240 acres
along Baltimore's 42-mile-long shoreline. It is a
combination of improvements to public cultural and
recreational amenities, new and rehabilitated housing,
retail spaces, and other commercial establishments.

While projects such as the Inner Harbor are lauded as
symbols of the city's renaissance, they are not without
their critics. Opponents to Harbor Place, a component of the
Inner Harbor, succeeded in getting the city to hold a
referendum on the project in 1978; but voters gave it their
approval. Others criticized the city's extensive use of
federal funds--especially UDAGs (Urban Development Action
Grants)--to aid commercial development. City officials
answer those who charge neighborhood neglect by saying that
at least as much money has been spent on innovative
neighborhood housing programs as on downtown renovation.

Baltimore was a pioneer in the neighborhood
rehabilitation and conservation efforts that became an
integral part of federal legislation in 1954. In the
Baltimore Pilot Area (1951-53). There was a three-pronged
attack on substandard housing: systematic housing inspection
and enforcement of city codes; the effecting of attitude
change toward blight by "rehabilitating the people"; and a
nonprofit revolving loan fund for homeowners unable to
obtain conventional financing.[23]

Strong community pressure in the 1950s prompted the
creation of a Housing Court that dealt with offenses related
to housing, health, and associated charges. Through
legislative enactment, it was later incorporated into the
municipal court system. An early civic mechanism for dealing
with housing decay gave Baltimore an advantage in slowing
down the deterioration of older buildings and
neighborhoods.[24]

Pioneering initiatives in urban homesteading and
"shopsteading" (a similar concept applied to commercial
buildings) have enhanced the Baltimore housing program's
reputation for innovation. Unique aspects of DHCD's efforts
include: locally funded rehabilitation loan and grant
programs for residential property owners; recycling older
buildings (e.g., schools) for adaptive reuse as housing; and
utilizing local tax-exempt bonds to finance low-interest
rate mortgages for eligible families.[25]

DETROIT

General Description

Detroit covers an area of approximately 139.6 square
miles--about 13,000 city blocks. The city began losing
population after 1950, at the same time that the black

population--attracted by economic opportunities in the booming automobile industry--increased. Federal government policies that promoted suburbanization through freeway construction and FHA and VA mortgage programs helped to promote the movement of the white middle class away from the city. Neighborhood stability has been a major casualty of the population turnover and decline. Patterns of residential segregation have long marked Detroit and its metropolitan area. One urbanist observed that the expansion of black residential areas was carefully controlled in cities through urban renewal condemnations and freeway construction.[26]

Local Political Culture

Detroit has home-rule power under the state of Michigan and a long tradition of reform. The charter of 1918 replaced the ward system of forty-two City Council members with nine members elected at-large. Charter revisions adopted in 1973 strengthened the mayor's power vis-a-vis the city council. The first beneficiary of this change was a black mayor-- Coleman Young--although the revisions were developed largely by white reformist commissioners.

Detroit has a strong mayor form of government. The city council has little power compared to the mayor. The mayor and the city council are elected to four-year terms in nonpartisan races. The mayor appoints administrative department heads; most municipal jobs are filled through the civil service process. The Detroit public school system operates autonomously from the city government under an elected governing board.

Eisinger notes that "the problem of race relations has run like a thick rope through the finer weave of politics" in Detroit. In many ways, race has been and still is the overriding issue in local politics and government. Joseph Drew found that race has been a prevailing issue in police-community relations, municipal employment, and redistribution of services as political issues. Police brutality is conventionally accepted as a cause of the riots that erupted in 1967 and as a major issue in the 1973 election of Coleman Young as Detroit's first black mayor--a position he still holds as the longest serving mayor in the city's history.[27]

"Detroit is the home of ethnic groups from places as exotic as the Chaldean region of Iraq and as familiar to the American experience as Poland and Italy. It is a blue collar town of tough sensibilities. . . ."[28] The cultural composition creates diversity in the city and contributes to dispersion of political power. Detroit lacks the organizational development and geographic linkages that support the formal party apparatus in machine cities. The reform model precludes this. Reform reduced the influence of political parties in local elections and as a consequence, allegiance is usually to individuals. In a city as diverse as Detroit, the result is extreme political fragmentation. Detroit has hundreds of active, community-based

organizations that compete for the decreasing largesse
offered by the city. Their only point of access into the
decision-making process is through informal relationships
with the mayor or city council.[29]

Informal political linkages are critical to
understanding Detroit's political culture. Local black
churches and the United Auto Workers (UAW), headquartered in
Detroit, are key elements. It was through the black churches
that Mayor Young generated a substantial bloc of continual
community support during elections as well as for policy
issues.[30]

After World War II, blacks played an increasing role in
shaky coalitions in local mayoral contests. Others in the
coalitions included the CIO and white liberals. The UAW,
among labor unions, had given unprecedented support to
progressive causes that improved working conditions for
blacks and that promoted some semblance of racial equality.
But progress within the ranks of the UAW has not been
without obstacles. Rising as he did through its ranks, Mayor
Young has had strong UAW support. He enjoyed it in his early
state legislature pursuits and in his early ascendancy as
the longest-serving mayor in Detroit history.

Prior to his election in 1973, proportionate black
representation in local government was actually and
perceptually underachieved. The black population constituted
16 percent of the total population in 1950; 29 percent in
1960. Until 1973, there were few black gains in local
government: only four black councilmen served from 1957 to
1965. The election of Jerome Cavanaugh in 1961 placed blacks
on the winning side of one mayoral election before Young.
Cavanaugh openly supported and presided over the War on
Poverty, but black representation in government remained
minimal. His political fate changed as a result of the 1967
riots, near the end of his last term. With his potential as
a Democratic presidential contender dashed, Cavanaugh
dedided not to run for the mayoralty again in 1969. Roman
Gribbs' subsequent election in 1969 (over Richard Austin,
the first black contender for the mayor's office), fueled
skepticism among the black population that equity could be
achieved in local elections. Gribbs had pictured himself as
a "transitional mayor," helping to prepare the city for
black rule.[31]

The city's population change ultimately affected the
city council makeup. The council is now far more
representative of and more receptive to the demands of
neighborhood activists.[32] Blacks comprised 65 percent of the
total population in 1980; five of nine city council members
were black. The Young administration worked to make the
police department and appointive offices more reflective of
the city's racial constituency.

Mayor Young has been called "a master of coalition
politics," a phrase indicative of the organizations existing
in Detroit with local power brokers as members. New Detroit,
the major civic organization, and Detroit Renaissance, the
business community's elite economic development group, are
among those that provide a forum for regular discussion

among local leaders and who promoted revitalization efforts.
The mayor has also been the major architect--as well as the
principal political beneficiary--of a federally funded
electoral coalition.[33] To cope with fiscal stress, Detroit
has garnered state and local government aid through a
combination of political acumen and bureaucratic competence.
Mayor Young has forged important political alliances in
Lansing and Washington and these reaped desirable outcomes
in federal and state aid packages during the 1970s.[34]

     Fiscal Condition

     As a result of changes in the Detroit city charter,
Coleman Young has direct control over government fiscal
purchases. The Budget Department, an executive department
with a director appointed by the mayor, prepares the capital
agenda and the capital and annual budgets for the city in
conjunction with Planning Director. The 1973 charter created
this department in recognition of its importance to the
chief executive's function. This arrangement became crucial
as the city addressed the fiscal crises of the 1970s and
1980s.

     In the cities, blacks are only elected to public
     office in appreciable numbers when the city is in
     economic decline because of the intense out-
     migration of middle- and upper-income whites.
     Property taxes and other funds raised from local
     revenues are inadequate to meet the demands for
     services within the cities. These factors have
     made the search for outside funds one of the most
     important and time-consuming functions of urban
     black elected officials.[35]

This excerpt may accurately depict the situation when Mayor
Young assumed the helm of government in Detroit.
     Detroit has been particularly hard hit by the structural
unemployment associated with the automobile industry's
decline. Population losses--including losses of upper- and
middle-income households--have likewise created a financial
drain; loss in tax revenue and a larger proportion of
dependent citizens have resulted. The intermittent
migration of businesses from the city, without a concomitant
in-migration, has also eroded the tax base. The use of tax
abatements to attract business or as a condition of business
has deprived the city of immediate anticipated revenues from
new developments. These incentives have not escape the
criticism of residents and politicians.
     Mayor Young took drastic steps to address a deficit that
has reached $61 million in 1978. Layoffs of municipal
employees--including fire fighters and police officers,
occurred--and a temporary hiring freeze was adopted. Police
layoffs reached one thousand; four thousand city employees
were cut overall in 1980. The police force was reduced by 27
percent between 1977 and 1981.[36] Programs and services were

cut: public transportation, public works, and museums
suffered.
     Since assuming office, Mayor Young has been concerned
with economic and industrial development, which have not
been without controversy. The Renaissance Center--an
occasionally troubled complex of office towers, a hotel, and
shops--was opened in 1977 by a coalition of business
interests. The construction of Central Industrial Park (also
known as Poletown) generated criticism and discontent as the
result of relocating area residents, businesses, and
institutions to clear land. The General Motors New Center
Area Development offered rehabilitated single-family
dwellings, town houses, and condominiums to lure the middle-
and upper-income groups back into the city and drew charges
of "gentrification." The Renaissance Center proved to be a
slow catalyst for downtown development.   Spin-off projects
completed are the Joe Louis Arena, Riverfront West luxury
apartments, the Millender Center complex, and the Omni
Hotel.
     Teetering toward financial collapse in 1981, Detroit had
a credit rating so low that Wall Street no longer considered
the city's bonds a sound investment. Moody's Bond Rating
Service lowered Detroit's municipal bond rating from "Baa"
to "Ba," which is considered to be below investment grade.[37]
In 1981, the mayor successfully garnered support from many
quarters to pass a financial survival package to rescue the
city from insolvency. At that point, the city was faced with
a $119.6 million deficit from the previous fiscal year and
$150 million for the upcoming fiscal year.   The three-part
survival package included: a city income tax increase on
residents and commuters; wage concessions by city employees;
and authorization to sell up to $125 million in deficit-
financing bonds.   The Michigan legislature's approval was
required to vote on the income tax.   The state legislation
required that unions take a two-year wage freeze befor the
tax could be collected. Voters approved the tax increase;
the unions reluctantly agreed to concessions, under the
threat of layoffs large enough to produce the equivalent
savings.[38] The ten-year bonds in the amount of $113 million
were sold to two city pension funds and local banks.
Although no similar crises have occurred since 1981, high
unemployment and low levels of service remain a part of
Detroit's fiscal landscape.

Housing and Community Development Setting

     The 1974 charter integrated planning and urban renewal
into the executive branch under the mayor. Previously, both
functions had been carried out semi-independently of each
other and of the mayor. The Community and Economic
Development Department (CEDD) resulted from the charter,
which required only that community development and economic
development be undertaken; but not necessarily in one
department.

CEDD initiates, implements, and administers all of Detroit's community development projects and programs. Among its activities are planning, zoning, and inspection as related to certain rehabilitation and construction programs. CEDD has shared overlapping functions with other city departments. Detroit also maintains a planning department, a zoning board of appeals and a department of buildings and safety engineering. CEDD manages all CDBG-funded projects in the city, matters related to neighborhood conservation, and city-owned property. The planning department is responsible for preparing the CDBG application--the major source of housing program dollars.

Until the latest charter revision, the Detroit housing department operated as the Detroit Housing Commission. It is governed by a nine-member housing commission, with five members appointed by the mayor and the others selected by community-based interests. The housing department manages the operation of some 11,000 units of public housing in the city. Before the new charter was implemented, the housing commission also managed urban renewal activities.

A number of public/private partnership agencies have taken the form of private, nonprofit corporations engaged in economic development planning and delivery. The Detroit Economic Growth Corporation (DEGC) serves under contract as a consultant to, and agency for, Detroit city government. The mayor appoints its fifty-five member board. The Economic Development Corporation, with a primary objective of alleviating unemployment and strengthening the economy, consists of a ten-member board appointed and chaired by the mayor. The Downtown Development Authority plans and implements projects in the central business district; its board of nine in also chaired and appointed by the mayor.

As in many cities, Detroit's housing policy has been strongly influenced by federal policy. During the 1950s and early 1960s, when clearance and new construction were in favor, urban renewal projects cleared many older homes in the near downtown area. Large-scale displacement of residents occurred in urban renewal areas now known as Lafayette Park and Elmwood Park, where developers built luxury apartments and town houses. Protests led to the later construction of some moderate-income and subsidized developments in those areas. As federal program priorities changed over time, emphasis shifted to the rehabilitation of existing structures. The out-migration of middle-income households during the late 1960s and 1970s provided basically sound housing stock that encouraged this approach over new construction.

Renovation of older homes has occurred to a very limited degree in Detroit. The city still has a very high rate of housing demolitions, and in many neighborhoods blighting influences are not yet stabilized.[39] Crime and perceived inadequacies of Detroit schools have reduced the residential demand in the city. Red-lining by mortgage banks and insurance companies has constrained neighborhood development as well.

An early attempt to rehabilitate and stabilize neighborhoods had some unanticipated and long-lasting negative consequences in Detroit. The city suffered the most adverse effects of the HUD Section 235 Program in the country. This program, to facilitate low-income home ownership through mortgage payment, was initially promoted by HUD officials in Detroit. The rehabilitation of existing structures was stressed and HUD wanted housing insurable under the low-income program to be produced quickly. The regional office was willing to allow substantial profits to speculators who did the actual purchase and rehabilitation work. Speculators purchased houses in unstable neighborhoods; cosmetically improved structures were overappraised; and excessive profits were made. The approval of mortgage insurance on a great number of houses with major defects created many problems. Homeowners with marginal incomes--faced with major repairs and little equity--frequently abandoned their homes. By the end of February 1975, HUD owned more than 16,000 mostly vacant structures in Detroit. It also held more than 4,000 vacant lots--which represented 4,000 demolished buildings.[40]

HUD and the city of Detroit have labored with the aftereffects of this program during the past several years. While abandoned structures in neighborhoods have undoubtedly contributed to blighting conditions, they have also provided an opportunity for large-scale redevelopment in some areas.

Among its current offerings, CEDD lists thirteen housing rehabilitation programs. CDBG is the primary funding source, although Michigan State Housing Development Authority also funds some programs. CDBG funds are used for low-interest loans, deferred loans, self-abating loans, and outright grants. Limited success has resulted in leveraging private dollars in rehabilitation programs. The programs also vary in scope, from targeted neighborhoods to city-wide areas, and include residential (one to four units) as well as commercial (five or more units) structures.

Severely impacted in the aftermath of the HUD Section 235 Program, Detroit's housing situation is recovering slowly--hampered by the lack of a well-coordinated and executed recovery plan. Faced with a number of concurrent problems, including loss of revenue-producing businesses and residents and limited resources, the city has not given neighborhood development a singular focus. No special-purpose entity has been established to pursue housing solutions as has been the case with economic and commercial development. That responsibility remains vested in a traditional line organizational configuration divided along functional lines among city departments.

PHILADELPHIA

General Background

Philadelphia covers an area of approximately 129 square miles.   The city's population has declined gradually since 1950 when it peaked at 2,071,605.   The 1980 population, signifying a loss of over   383,000 persons,   fell to 1,688,210. The 1980 black population comprised 41 percent. Philadelphia is composed of ethnic populations that tend to cluster in specific geographic areas. In South Philadelphia, one finds the Italians and the Irish; in North Philadelphia, the Poles;   in West Philadelphia,   the Ukrainians and the blacks; in the Northeast, the Jews.[41]

Fifty-eight percent of the city's 685,271 housing units were built before 1939. Philadelphia is primarily a city of row houses   and small   structures,   mostly   of masonry construction.   In 1974,   only 16 percent of the residential housing stock was concentrated in structures containing five or more units. This housing stock configuration of single-family attached masonry housing held high rehabilitation potential.[42]

Local Political Culture

Philadelphia has a home rule charter that sets forth the organization,   powers,   and duties of its officers and agencies.   Philadelphia government is composed of the city government,   the school district,   the judicial government, special-purpose   units,   and independent   boards   and commissions. The school district operates independently of the city government, although the mayor appoints its nine-member board.

The 1951 home rule charter established the strong mayor form of government in Philadelphia. The mayor's stay in office is limited to two successive terms.   The seventeen-member city council in a bilateral process, has one member elected from each of ten councilmanic districts and seven from the city at-large. Each political party may nominate one candidate for each of the ten district offices but only five candidates for the seven at-large positions. Each voter may cast a ballot for one district council member and five of the seven at-large positions. This system is intended to assure representation of the minority political party (in a two-party system) in at least two at-large seats. Council members serve four-year terms concurrent with the mayor's term.

Philadelphia's long history of   reform has been influenced by party politics. Reform began in 1948 as the result of municipal corruption.   The Greater Philadelphia Movement formed that year was a coalition group through which the business and civic elite became involved in major social problems, · including housing. In the 1950s, under

Mayors Joseph S. Clark and J. Richardson Dilworth, planning and good government approaches united many interests and reversed Philadelphia's decay. When James H. G. Tate, a product of the Democratic party machine, assumed the position of mayor in 1962, he attempted to consolidate power and influence in himself and the city administration.[43]

Mayor Tate, a prophet without honor, was quickly disregarded by liberal reformers after his election and fell equally afoul of the business community--primarily because of his pro-labor union policies. Tate became known as an effective leader of the municipal reform groups that eventually pressured Congress into passing the Revenue Sharing Act.

The Tate administration engaged in two noteworthy efforts purportedly to solve the problems of poverty in the black community. One was to aggressively encourage the redevelopment of Center City so that the tax revenues produced would help bolster immigrant blacks and extend renewal to the slum areas themselves. The second effort was to construct low-cost housing or renovate existing units in North Philadelphia under urban renewal. Neither approach succeeded. Instead urban renewal displaced many poor- and working-class families in North Philadelphia. some fled to neighborhoods farther north whose white population, in turn, fled from them. The same phenomenon occurred, somewhat less virulently, in West Philadelphia. Poor residents came to occupy the housing once owned by the black homeowners. Lending institutions were increasingly unwilling to provide mortgage money or reconstruction loans, which further enforced neighborhood decline.[44]

In late 1970, Tate--forbidden by the home rule charter to seek a third term, endorsed Frank Rizzo as his successor (he later called this the worst mistake he ever made). As police commissioner, Rizzo was controversial: he made headlines in the late 1960s when he raided poetry readings at local coffeehouses and later when he demanded that the city buy armed tanks to patrol black neighborhoods, guns pointing at people. Most blacks and liberal whites detested him. In the 1972 election, despite nearly unanimous opposition of the city's black population (about one-third of all registered voters); Rizzo was elected mayor by a comfortable margin. He became a hero in white, working-class wards, serving the maximum allowable two terms. A charter amendment that would have allowed him to seek a third term was defeated. Party politics, and its corollaries of patronage and dependence, prevailed until William Green's election in 1980.

Green brought a team of good-government types with him. Son of Philadelphia's longtime Democratic boss and a wealthy former congressman, he was labeled the candidate of the city's liberal reformists.[45] During his campaign, he indicated that he would quickly reverse Rizzo's policy on two highly sensitive issues: the relationship of blacks and the police department and neighborhood housing desegregation. He appointed thirty blacks, including his successor, W. Wilson Goode, to high administrative posts. Many were surprised when Green announced plans not to seek a second term for personal reasons. At the time, he was enjoying what most observers viewed as a political upswing.[46] Under an administration where the buzzwords were efficiency and frugality, the deficit Green had inherited was transformed into a 40 million surplus within a year.[47] Green's fiscal conservatism and social liberalism has been termed New Fiscal Populism.[48]

The political progress of black Philadelphians has been slower than in cities where they make up a larger part of the population.   During Green's tenure, blacks reached a more equitable representation--six of seventeen members--on the city council. Joseph Coleman, an early homesteading advocate, was elected president. Wilson Goode, as managing director, became the city's top-appointed executive and the highest-ranking black official. He succeeded Green in 1984 to become the city's first black mayor.

Wilson Goode assumed the mayoralty faced with the problems common to other large cities. His previous experience in the Green cabinet initially proved to be an advantage as he tackled his first issues, which included jobs, union contracts, the cable TV system, and relationships with the city council.

Besides his experience in the Green administration, Goode had distinctive credentials.   He headed the Philadelphia Council for Community Advancement and was director of the state's Public Utility Commission.   Goode's background was apparently an major asset in pursuing the backing of the business community during his mayoral campaign.   Mayor Goode was elected on a platform of government efficiency, racial harmony, and goodwill.   After assuming office, his political posture seemed to improve as the city bounced back from a decade of decline.   Democratic presidential candidate Walter Mondale even interviewed him for the vice-presidential spot in 1984.

Mayor Goode's record was tainted in May 1985 when the headquarters of the organization Move, considered as radical, was destroyed.   In that incident, Philadelphia police bombed the building, resulting in the deaths of eleven people, including four children.   Fifty-three homes were destroyed and another eight were heavily damaged. Mayor Goode was severely criticized by parts of the black community but praised by others, including U.S. Attorney General Edwin Meese.   After hearings held by a panel appointed to investigate the confrontation, the mayor was found grossly negligent in handling the incident. Criticism seemed to plague his administration after that point. Even efforts to rebuild the homes of the fire victims were bothered with controversy and allegations of improprieties. In March 1986, the first residents returned to their new town houses built by the city.

Despite the political costs of the previous few years, Mayor Goode defeated former Mayor Frank Rizzo, who again challenged him for the mayoralty.   Rizzo had lost to Goode in the Democratic primary four years hence.   In 1987, he switched parties, won the Republican primary, and ran against Goode in the general election. Goode's victory with just 51% of the vote over Rizzo's 49% is probably indicative of the loss of popularity and support among blacks and whites after his first-term imbroglio.

Fiscal Condition

The mayor appoints a director of finance. The city controller is elected and responsible for a pre-audit and post-audit of the city and school district. The city provides the usual array of municipal services and also owns the gas works, which is operated by a nonprofit corporation.

The city is coterminous with the county and the independent school district. Besides the school board, a number of other agencies operate or overlap in the city-county authority; these include the Philadelphia Redevelopment Authority and the Housing Authority. The proportion of common-function workers per 1,000 residents was the highest of the large cities in 1976, as were the costs for services.[49] This city is faced with the challenge of reducing expenditures while at the same time dealing with pressure for wage increases, court-mandated pension contributions, and an older and poorer citizenry that requires more services.

Despite job and population losses typical of most large, older, industrial cities, Philadelphia balanced its books until 1975. Its operating deficit that year was $31 million--which increased to $90.1 million in 1976.[50] Between 1972 and 1976, total operating expenditures rose faster than revenues. The city was particularly vulnerable to political decisions and economic events beyond its control because the revenue base was quite diversified. In 1976, property taxes--which had declined since 1972--accounted for 11.5 percent of total operating funds. An overlapping burden has been the even more drastic increase in school district expenditures versus those in the city. The school district's poor fiscal condition arises from a 40 percent increase in wages and benefits and a 10 percent decline in school enrollment between 1972 and 1976. Property taxes and other own-source revenue accounted for only 37 percent of total revenues for the school district versus 65 percent for the city in 1976.

Police commissioner for seven years immediately prior to becoming mayor, Rizzo apparently gave the police department special attention while in the office. A study by the Citizens Crime Commission of Philadelphia found that the city had twenty-eight thousand police officers--more per capita than Los Angeles or New York. The city was also spending more on police per capita than the other two cities, had more squad cars, and replaced them more frequently. The city's crime rate was also appreciably lower than in New York and Los Angeles. In 1979, however, the Justice Department filed suit against the city, charging widespread and systematic police brutality against blacks.

The case was dismissed on the grounds that the federal
government lacked jurisdiction.[51]

When Green assumed the reins of Philadelphia government,
he inherited a city on the threshold of budget deficits and
municipal cutbacks. Within seven weeks of being sworn in, he
discovered that the deficit was not $7.6 million, as Rizzo
had stated, but at least $167 million by the end of the
upcoming fiscal year on June 30, 1981.[52] Standard and Poor's
bond-rating service lowered the city's bond rating from from
"A" to "triple B-Plus," citing Philadelphia's limited
revenue-raising potential and high levels of public spending
as reasons for the action. The city was in need of capital
improvements to its aged physical plant, and this rating
added to the cost of capital borrowing. Cutbacks and poor
service in public transportation had already been
experienced.

Actions taken by Green's administration to handle the
deficit included laying off over a thousand municipal
employees, increasing real estate taxes, and raising transit
fares. Green was also able to negotiate a zero percent wage-
increase contract with all city employees--except police--in
1980. He is generally acknowledged for leading a virtual
revolution in municipal administration with the appointment
of efficiency-oriented technocrats. But when Goode became
mayor, issues of limited economic resources versus unlimited
demands continued to plague city government.

Housing and Community Development Setting

It has been said that the administrations of the recent
past have had no housing policy in Philadelphia.[53] Since the
election of Wilson Goode, a broad statement of housing
policy has been formulated under the Director of Housing.
The policy, issued in 1984, identified the following
priorities based on need: the homeless, public housing,
owner-occupied, private rental and vacant housing, and new
construction. The current organizational structure places
the director in the mayor's cabinet. Directly accountable
to the Director are four departments: the Office for Housing
and Community Development (OHCD); the Redevelopment
Authority (RA); the Philadelphia Housing Authority (PHA);
and the Philadelphia Housing Development Corporation (PHDC).

Internal and external conditions led to the
establishment of Philadelphia's Office of OHCD in 1976, a
response to the federal government's consolidation of
numerous categorical grants into the Community Development
Block Grant. OHCD's primary charge is to manage the block
grant funds; it also coordinates and manages the city's
housing and community development programs, which had
previously been undertaken by several agencies. To enhance
coordination, OHCD was placed under the mayor's office,
where it has both policy functions and implementation
responsibilities.

OHCD coordinates the activities of the PHA and other
smaller agencies with those of city departments. It

prepares the annual application for CDBG and other federal funds, for state housing funds, and integrates the activities with other community development efforts. OHCD works with other agencies, including the Philadelphia Industrial Development Corporation (PIDC), Philadelphia City Planning Commission, the city's Commerce Department, and others in planning, funding, and management of major economic development projects.

Philadelphia has several special-purpose organizations that collaborate with OHCD. Organized in 1977, the Philadelphia Citywide Development Corporation (PCDC) administers and oversees business and commercial development in most areas of the city in conjuction with OHCD, its primary source of funds. Established in 1945, the RA strives to replace blighted areas with socially and economically sound projects to fulfill the city's needs for housing, economic development, and tax-ratables to pay for continuing, needed services. The RA is directed by an unpaid board of five members, appointed by the mayor to overlapping five-year terms. The authority carries out certain activities for OHCD such as site improvements, relocation services, and land development.

The PHDC was chartered as a nonprofit corporation in 1965 to promote and develop housing for low- and moderate-income families in Philadelphia by working cooperatively with housing and renewal agencies and with local community interests. The mayor appoints the board of directors, which consists of ten Philadelphia city officials and twenty-five community representatives. An executive committee of fifteen directors handles ongoing policy matters; the executive vice president handles corporation activities. PHDC receives one-half of Philadelphia's community development budget.[54]

PHDC administers the Urban Homesteading Program in Philadelphia. Its placement there implicitly targets the low- and moderate-income population. PHDC has previously undertaken production of new single-family housing for low-and moderate-income families under Sections 235 and 236; it now administers a number of other programs for OHCD, including one to rehabilitate vacant properties and sell them at prevailing market rates with CDBG subsidization. Another home buyer selection service advises low- and moderate-income families anticipating homeownership.

The PHA manages more than 22,500 units of public housing in the city. It was created in 1937 under Pennsylvania Authorities Law--independent of city government--as a nonprofit, quasi-public corporation. Overall direction of the PHA is the responsibility of a five-member board that serves without compensation for five-year terms. The mayor and city controller each appoint two of the members; the fifth is selected by the four.

The politics of Philadelphia government have been replicated in the politics of housing and community development. Racial divisiveness and conflict have surfaced in relation to housing policy and community development. A report by the Philadelphia Urban League on the problems of blacks found that the city remained divided by race, geography, and economics.[55] The report found that the black unemployment rate was among the highest in major cities (16.3 percent, compared to 4.5 percent among white Philadelphians) and that housing policies had eliminated 8,000 units, most of them in black neighborhoods.

Charges of displacement and gentrification further reveal this tension. Mayor Joseph S. Clark, elected in 1952, and his ally and successor, J. Richardson Dilworth, were liberal Democrats who initiated urban renewal in Philadelphia. The Society Hill neighborhood development is noted as one of the first to attract upper-income white households to a declining Central City. Mayor Dilworth admitted that the revival of Society Hill was a deliberate attempt to "get white leadership back."[56] City administrators were accused of supporting the movement, which was seen as harmful to lower-income residents. Mistakenly described by some as an urban homesteading project, Society Hill residents could receive low-interest loans to rehabilitate their properties from the city.

Charges of gentrification seem more legitimate in Philadelphia than in either Detroit or Baltimore. The restoration of town houses in Society Hill displaced old ethnic communities.[57] South of Society Hill is Queen Village, also marked by gentrification. The black population in the area dropped from nearly 50 percent in 1970 to less than 25 percent in 1980. Poorer blacks and members of other ethnic groups were displaced by rising property values and taxes and an influx of young professionals, who restored the existing old town houses and built new ones.[58] On the other hand, blacks made gains during the administrations of Clark and Dilworth in municipal employment (from few in 1952 to 30 percent by 1962); home ownership (from 29 percent in 1950 to 44 percent by 1966); and housing standards (66 percent lived in code shelter in 1950; 85 percent did by 1960).[59]

The twenty-year saga of the construction of the Whitman Park Townhouse project further portrays the community development environment Whitman Park was originally proposed in the mid-1950s as a high-rise rise public housing development in a predominantly white South Philadelphia neighborhood. By the time design began--ten years later--HUD had abandoned vertical housing in favor of town houses. Residents of the heavily ethnic neighborhood opposed the project, as did Mayor Rizzo, who announced that Whitman Park would never be built while he was in office. In 1975, a federal district judge ruled that the delays were racially motivated and ordered the construction to proceed. When the project opened in 1982, only 58 of the 120 units had been built, the result of continued oppositon.[60]

Citing Mayor Rizzo's oppositon to Whitman Park, HUD withheld more than $63 million in CDBG funds in May 1979 (they were later restored). Rizzo's stance apparently contributed to Philadelphia being eliminated from consideration for $21 million in Urban Development Grant (UDAG) funds intended to aid distressed communities.[61]

Neighborhood housing desegregation was high among Mayor Green's priorities upon assuming office. The city's housing

office,   plagued with instability,   had seen five directors
between 1974 and 1980. OHDC troubles began with the scandal-
plagued Model Cities program,   which it was created to
replace.   The office faced charges that it was ridden by
patronage appointments and   incompetence.   Housing activists
vociferously denounced Philadelphia's emphasis on downtown
redevelopment at the expense of decaying neighborhoods.   In
1978,   the head of the city's Urban Homesteading Program was
jailed for extorting money and personal housing improvements
from city contractors.   When Green became mayor, housing was
a major political and social issue; 30,000 abandoned housing
units   and   more   than 400   formally designated distressed
neighborhoods existed.[62]
     Philadelphia has   responded to community pressure as
related to housing. On the matter of squatting, Philadelphia
has been a forerunner in accommodating those persons who
take up unauthorized residence in abandoned properties.[63]
After   officials hesitated to evict them,   squatters were
given   title to the houses they occupied in more than
seventy cases.[64] A group known as the Inner-City Organizing
Network served as the sqatters' agents, helping them to cut
through red tape and occupy the housing.   The city council
adopted an ordinance creating the 1202A Emergency Nuisance
Abatement Program in 1982;   it provides administrative
sanction and support for squatting within the guidelines
spelled out by the program. This program is also operated by
PHDC under contract with the OHDC, which attempts to secure
ownership for the sqatter but makes no guarantees.   Housing
activists advocating this program complained that previous
government programs to put homes back into the hands of the
public worked too slowly.[65]

CONCLUSION

     Baltimore,   Detroit,   and Philadelphia faced unique
circumstances prior to and during the years of urban
homesteading implementation.   Characteristics of the three
cities are summarized in Table 5.4.   Fiscal problems have
dominated the public agenda in the three cities recently.
And each has undertaken various cutback measures to address
them. The political environments have determined the sources
of financial support for each city.   Baltimore enjoyed
significant assistance from the local business and financial
community and state government.   Detroit has struggled with
marginal private sector support and hefty federal aid
dollars.   Philadelphia has experienced wavering private
support and major reductions in public expenditures.
     The community development settings for the cities vary
significantly. Baltimore has an   umbrella agency   to
coordinate all housing and community development activities
and has acquired a national reputation for innovation and
comprehensiveness. Although consolidation of some activities
has occurred since 1970, Detroit's CEDD continues to share
housing- and community-development responsibility with other

TABLE 5.4
SUMMARY OF CHARACTERISTICS

CHARACTERISTIC	BALTIMORE	DETROIT	PHILADELPHIA
Local governance	Mayor-Council Council elected by joint at-large and district system	Mayor-Council Council elected at-large	Mayor-Council Council elected by joint at-large and district system
Community Development Setting	Umbrella, centralized agency responsible for all housing and community development functions; city department	Agency with shared and overlapping functions administers all community development projects and programs; city department	Quasi-public organization handles implementation for city government
Urban Homesteading Agency	Department of Housing and Community Development	Community and Economic Development Department	Office of Housing and Community Development
Sources of Support for Community Development	Local business and financial communities, state government, federal grants-in-aid	Hefty federal grants-in-aid; marginal private support	Increasing amounts of federal-grants-in-aid; waivering private support
Population Trend	Decreasing since 1950	Decreasing since 1950	Decreasing since 1950
1980 Black Population	56%	65%	41%
1980 Poverty Level	22.9%	21.9%	20.6%

city agencies.   Philadelphia has   delegated a   considerable
amount of its housing- and community-development function to
quasi-public organizations through contractual arrangements.
The   structures   for   carrying   out   urban   homesteading
activities as well as the sources of political and financial
suppport are   determinants of program outcomes.
     Detroit instituted more structural political reform than
Baltimore or   Philadelphia.   Although all three   cities have
mayor-council governments,   Baltimore and Philadelphia also
have partisan   elections   and   a   mixed-district/at-large
constituency   arrangement.   Political   scientists disagree
about the potential policy consequences of urban political
structures.   Banfield and Wilson's widely   known   thesis
suggests   that cities   dominated by a middle-class public-
regarding ethos   may support greater   public expenditures.[66]
Their theory conflicts with other research which finds that
reformers wanted efficent, businesslike government with
lower levels of spending.   Still others have shown that
reform characteristics have little or no impact on municipal
spending   levels.[67] Research   on all three cities   revealed
increased spending levels--particularly in the last ten
years--was due to the growing demand for, and costs of, city
services.
     Formal   political   representation   and   community
organizations that play a role in community development
dynamics   varied   among   the   cities.   Baltimore   and
Philadelphia, from the standpoint of community development
and housing concerns, would probably be most responsive to
neighborhood input by virtue of district representation. "In
cities where party,   neighborhood,   or other parts of
political   organizations   are   relatively   well
established . . . and where local politics are relatively
visible, elected officials have a much stronger incentive to
worry about their current office . . . than in cities where
levels of political organization and participation are
lower."[68] Neighborhood groups are active and numerous in
Detroit and Baltimore;   party   politics are robust in
Philadelphia.   Organized groups can act to influence the
implementation of urban homesteading and other programs.   On
the other hand, mayors--as in Detroit and Baltimore--can
maximize   their influence when formal party politics are
weak.
     The power to propose a budget, to appoint and remove
department heads, and to veto acts of a city council are the
major sources of influence supported by the executive reform
movement for strong mayor-council governments.[69] Mayors in
Baltimore, Detroit, and Philadelphia possess formal powers
requisite to the exercise of influence.   Armed with such
potential influence, mayors in all three cities could exert
control over their community development/housing agencies as
well as   the urban-homesteading   implementing agencies.
Different patterns of influence existed in the three cities.
In Baltimore, Mayor Schaefer was a major agent in innovative
neighborhood redevelopment initiatives.   In Detroit, Mayor
Young wields major influence over housing redevelopment
efforts through   traditional city line agencies.   In

Philadelphia, mayoral control over some housing programs, including urban homesteading, is channeled through the extensive use of quasi-public organizations. In each case, mayoral input has affected program implementation to different degrees. The next two chapters present details of program operation and further explanation of local political involvement.

NOTES

1. Michael C.   D.   Macdonald, America's Cities: A Report on the Myth of Urban Renaissance (New York: Simon & Schuster,   1984),   p.   197.   The others were Newark and St. Louis.
2. Richard Ben Cramer,   "Can the Best Man Win?" Esquire 102 (October 1984), 57-72.
3. Raymond J. Struyk and David W. Rasmussen, A Housing Strategy for the City of Detroit (Washington,   D.C.:   Urban Institute Press, 1981).
4. Roberto Brambilla and Gianni Longo, Learning from Baltimore (New York: Institute for Environmental Action, 1979), p. 21.
5. Matthew A.   Crenson, Neighborhood Politics (Cambridge: Harvard University Press, 1983), p. 37.
6. Brambilla and Longo, Learning from Baltmore, p. 15.
7. The Regional Science Institute, Functional and Economic Interdependence in the Baltimore Region (Baltimore: Regional Planning Council, 1970), p. xiii.
8. Charles L.   Levine, Irene S.   Rubin,   and George G. Wolohojian, The Politics of Retrenchment (Beverly Hills, California: Sage Publications, 1981), p. 123.
9. Ibid.
10. Brambilla and Longo, Learning from Baltimore, pp. 23 and 131.
11. Washington Post, "Mayor Schaefer: Baltimore's Best," June 25, 1981, A-23.
12. Robert A.   Dahl, Who Governs?   (New Haven: Yale University Press,   1961),   p.   200, and Robert Salisbury, "Urban Politics: The New Convergence of Power," The Journal of Politics 26 (1964), 775-97.
13. Levine,   Rubin,   and Wolohojian, The Politics of Retrenchment, p. 14.
14. New York Times, April 19, 1976, p. 31.
15. Brambilla and Longo, Learning from Baltimore, p. 16.
16. Levine,   Rubin,   and Wolohojian, Politics of Retrenchment, p. 116.
17. Ibid.,   p.   119; International City Management Association, Municipal Year Book (Washington,   D.C.: International City Management Association,   1983),   p.   26; United States Department of Commerce,   Bureau of the Census, City Government Finances 1982-83 (Washington,   D.C.:   GPO, 1983).
18. Brambilla and Longo, Learning from Baltimore, p. 133.
19. Levine,   Rubin,   and Wolohojian, The Politics of

Retrenchment, p. 128.
    20. Crenson, Neighborhood Politics, p. 292.
    21. Mary K. Nenno and Paul C. Brophy, Housing and Local Government (Washington, D.C.: International City Management Association,1982), p. 202.
    22. Crenson, Neighborhood Politics, p. 36.
    23. John D. Heinberg,"The Evolution of Rehabilitation as Public Policy," in Housing Rehabilitation: Economic, Social and Policy Perspectives, David Listokin, ed. (New Brunswick, New Jersey: Rutgers University Press, 1983), p. 64.
    24. Brambilla and Longo, Learning from Baltimore, p. 36.
    25. Nenno and Brophy, Housing and Local Government, p. 203.
    26. Peter Eisinger, The Politics of Displacement: Racial and Ethnic Transition in Three American Cities (New York: Academic Press, 1970), p. 59.
    27. Eisinger, Politics of Displacement, p. 56; Joseph Drew, "Three Area Agencies; Government Contracting, Service Delivery and Bureaucratic Performance," Ph.D. diss., (Detroit: Wayne State University, 1982), p. 58.
    28. Eisinger, Politics of Displacement, p. 55.
    29. Drew, "Three Area Agencies," p. 57.
    30. Ibid.
    31. Eisinger, Politics of Displacement, p. 64.
    32. Lynn Bachelor and Bryan D. Jones, "Managed Participation: Detroit's Neighborhood Opportunity Fund," Journal of Applied Behavioral Science 17 (October-November 1981), 524.
    33. James W. Fossett, Federal Aid to Big Cities: The Politics of Dependence (Washington, D.C.: The Brookings Institution, 1983), p. 32. p. 32.
    34. Bryan D. Jones, "Decision at Milwaukee Junction: Community Leadership and Corporate Power", (unpublished manuscript) 1984, p. 10.
    35. William E. Nelson, Jr., and Winston Van Horne, "Black Elected Administrators," Public Administration Review 34 no. 6 (November/December 1974), 526-33.
    36. Macdonald, America's Cities, p. 312.
    37. Jones, "Decision at Milwaukee Junction," p. 5.
    38. The New York Times, July 30, 1981, p. 14.
    39. City of Detroit, "Annual Overall Economic Development Progress Report and Program Projection," June 30, 1983, IV-22.
    40. Mark Van Allsburg, "Property Abandonment in Detroit," Wayne Law Review 20 (March 1974), 861.
    41. From Peter O. Muller, et al., Metropolitan Philadelphia Conflicts and Social Cleavages (New York: Ballinger Publishing, 1976), as cited in Joseph Drew, p. 81.
    42. James W. Hughes and Kenneth D. Bleakly, Jr., Urban Homesteading (New Brunswick, New Jersey: The Center for Urban Policy Research, Rutgers University, 1975), p. 133.
    43. David Rogers, The Management of Big Cities (Beverly Hills, California: Sage Publications, 1971), pp. 75 and 84.
    44. John Guinther, Philadelphia: A Dream for the Keeping (Philadelphia: Continental Heritage Press, 1982),

p. 170.

45. The Washington Post, January 1, 1980, p. A2.

46. Ibid., November 3, 1982, p. A8.

47. Guinther, A Dream for the Keeping, p. 181.

48. Terry Nichols Clark, "Local Fiscal Dynamics Under Old and New Federalism, Urban Affairs Quarterly, 19 (September 1983), 67.

49. Henry L. Mortimer, "Philadelphia Case Study" (Washington, D.C.: Urban Institute, 1978), pp. 6 and 13.

50. Ibid., p. 1.

51. The New York Times, February 3, 1980, p. 27.

52. Ibid., February 24, 1980, p. 26.

53. Interview with Julia Robinson, Philadelphia Office of Housing, November 15, 1984.

54. Ibid.

55. The New York Times, February 11, 1982, p. 21.

56. Macdonald, America's Cities p. 278.

57. The New York Times, November 26, 1982, pp. 11-12.

58. The New York Times, August 7, 1983, p. 18.

59. Macdonald, America's Cities, p. 279.

60. The New York Times, November 28, 1982, p. 14.

61. The Washington Post, March 19, 1980, p. A16.

62. The New York Times, December 22, 1980, p. A20.

63. Squatting is defined as illegal occupation of government owned vacant housing or other abandoned housing.

64. The New York Times, January 13, 1981, p. A9.

65. Ibid.

66. James Q. Wilson and Edward C. Banfield, "Public Regardingness as a Value Premise in Voting Behavior," American Political Science Review 58 (December 1964), p. 885.

67. David R. Morgan and John P. Pelissero, "Urban Policy: Does Political Structure Matter?" The American Political Science Review 74 (December 1980) 1005.

68. Fossett, Federal Aid to Big Cities, pp. 28-29.

69. Glenn Abney and Thomas P. Lauth, "Influence of the Chief Executive on Line Agencies," Public Administration Review 42 (March/April 1982) 137.

6

Variations of Urban Homesteading Program Implementation

Surveys of Baltimore, Detroit, and Philadelphia confirm that they have similar socioeconomic, fiscal, and housing problems. The sources of these problems are also quite similar: deteriorating neighborhoods, emigration, loss of industry, and erosion of tax bases. The root causes of neighborhood decline are elusive, leading policymakers to try various approaches to reverse the process. Unquestionably, abandoned housing in each city contributes significantly to neighborhood blight and crime. The urban homesteading concept was advanced as a way to turn abandoned housing into an important resource.

The preferred use of vacant housing for urban homesteading is reflected in the cities' goals. Each exercised the discretion provided in Section 810 to establish an idiosyncratic policy goal; local conditions and housing/community development strategies influenced those goals. As might be expected, implementation varied among the cities.

This chapter analyzes and describes urban homesteading operations in Baltimore, Detroit, and Philadelphia. We will begin with a look at the organizational structures for implementation; program goals and objectives; and program characteristics. Next, the programmatic outputs of the programs will be considered, and finally, regulatory aspects of the federal and local programs will be compared.

IMPLEMENTATION IN THREE CITIES

Baltimore, Detroit, and Philadelphia carried out locally legislated Urban Homesteading Programs as well as the federal Section 810 Program. The local guidelines differed significantly from the federal. The local programs, free of federal directives, were presumably more reflective of local conditions. Components of urban homesteading implementation will be examined across programs to discern elements that may account for differences in outcome. Overall operation of the program in the subject cities is summarized in Table 6.1.

TABLE 6.1
URBAN HOMESTEADING PROGRAM SUMMARY

CATEGORY	BALTIMORE	DETROIT	PHILADELPHIA
City Characteristics	Innovator in housing and community development programs. Umbrella agency for all housing programs. Sec. 810 Program targeted in one neighborhood. Local program included scattered sites.	Some housing functions overlap with other agencies. Sec. 810 Program targeted in two neighborhoods for low- and moderate-income groups. Local program is citywide with no maximum income limits.	All housing rehabilitation carried out by non-profit organization. Designated blocks in two neighborhoods targeted in local and federal demonstration programs. The neighborhood targeted in Sec. 810 operating program focused on low- and moderate-income groups.
Program Goals	Attract middle-income households and revitalize tax base.	Promote low- and middle-income homeownership and stabilize neighborhoods.	Low- and moderate-income homeownership housing improvement.
Program Origination	Local: 1973 by Board of Estimates Federal: 1974 (demonstration) 1978 (operating)	Local: 1983 Federal: 1979 (operating)	Local: 1973 (by city ordinance; amended 1975) Federal: 1974 (demonstration) 1982(operating)

92

Administration	Urban Homestead Manager within City-Owned Property Management Unit of the Home Ownership Development Division under the Baltimore Department of Housing and Community Development	Urban Homestead Unit within the Housing Programs Division of the Detroit Community and Economic Development Department.	Originated in the Independent Urban Homesteading Board. Assumed by the Philadelphia Office of Housing and Community Development; later transferred to non-profit Philadelphia Housing Development Corporation.
Support Mechanisms	Homesteader associations	Repair workshops	Pre- and post-homeownership counseling. Mandatory home repair workshops.
Primary Financing Sources	Section 312 loans. City-financed low-interest loans.	Section 312 loans. CDBG-funded grants and loans.	Section 312 loans. Low-interest state-funded loans; foundations, CDBG-funded loans.

Baltimore's Local Homesteading Program

Baltimore's locally initiated Urban Homesteading Program emerged as one part of the efforts of the DHCD's Home Ownership Division. The DHCD's top priorities, in descending order, are: (1) neighborhood revitalization; (2) provision of low- and moderate-income housing; and (3) general housing improvement. The division aims to secure financing and assistance for prospective property rehabilitators. Attempts to reinterest the financial community in the central city area and to provide homeownership counseling have been made. The local homesteading effort required no special legislation because the DHCD was already responsible for the management of city-owned properties acquired through tax delinquency, abandonment, or foreclosure and finding new owners for them. These properties constituted the program's housing stock.

Baltimore attempted to address neighborhood deterioration comprehensively by focusing on vacant housing. When it began in 1973, Baltimore's Urban Homesteading Program had an inventory of 1,500 boarded-up properties under its management. Later in the 1970s city surplus properties reached a high of 2,500 due to abandonment, out-migration, and lack of capital to upgrade. The inventory of vacant housing held by HUD reached a high of 167 in September 1974.

Hughes, who studied the first homesteading cities, has labeled Baltimore officials "the well-directed homesteaders."[1] The DHCD's umbrella agency structure encompasses many of the operations essential to an Urban Homesteading Program. Rather than relying upon one staff to carry out all aspects of the program, the department can utilize the resources of other divisions: to evaluate vacant structures or arrange financing, for example. The staff, initially, consisted of eight people. A six-person board was established internally to make final decisions on staff actions. The board differed from the traditional model in its in-house composition of DHCD staff: (1) Chief of City-owned Properties, (2) Homesteading Manager, (3) Home Ownership Development Program Director, (4) Supervisor of Construction, (5) Home Ownership Counseling Manager, and (6) Head of Property Sales. DHCD utilized citizen participation to screen homesteaders; selection committees consisting of fair housing officials, community organizations, and staff determined eligibility prior to a lottery drawing for homesteads.

The local Urban Homesteading Program operated in three neighborhoods and some scattered sites. The scattered site units are all located within the central city area. Some lower-income households participated in the scattered sites component of the program, where instances of hands on rehabilitation or sweat equity and homesteaders acting as their own general contractors to cut costs were commonplace.

The units found most suitable for homesteading were the small- to moderate-size row houses, which could be rehabilitated at modest cost. However, larger, formerly

elegant dwellings   attracted the most   affluent participants
and sparked   the initial positive press   releases.[2] Stirling
Street,   the first urban homesteading   area,   is situated in
the Oldtown   Urban Renewal   Area.   The   block consisted   of
forty-two row   houses slated   for clearance   before protests
proclaimed   their architectural   and historic   significance.
Utilizing urban   homesteading,   the   forty-two homes   were
combined into twenty-five and renovated.   Barre Circle, the
second   urban homesteading   target,   consisted   of 125   mid-
nineteenth century row   houses in   the Fremont Urban Renewal
Area.   Prior   to homesteading,   citizen protests   there had
diverted plans   for clearance for highway construction.
     Otterbein,   the   third   site,   is   located adjacent   to
downtown within   the Inner Harbor   West Urban   Renewal Area.
The   113 mid-19th   century rowhouses   vary in   architectural
style and size ranging from small (ten and twelve feet wide)
to   some   large   enough   for   conversion   into   apartments.
Rehabilitation   costs   ranged   from $14,500   to   just   over
$50,000.   In   addition to supervision   by DHCD,   plans for
exterior work were subject to   review and endorsement by the
Otterbein   Architectural   Review   Committee   (ARC).   ARC
consisted   of   community-elected   and   DHCD-designated
homesteaders   to   enforce   design   standards   that   had   been
jointly set by the Otterbein homesteaders and the city.
     The local Urban Homesteading   Program's objective was to
retain   and   attract middle-class   residents.   The   target
population,   as such,   were the working and middle class who
could   afford   the   costs   of   rehabilitation   or   had   the
requisite   repair   skills.   The   availability   of   low-cost
financing for   high-quality residential   structures was   the
ostensible appeal of the program.
     "The   political   game   plan   was   to   create   a   new
neighborhood and   newness in the   Inner Harbor   and increase
the   tax   base."[3]   Such   is   the   strategy   outlined   in   an
interview with   a DHCD   official about   the Otterbein   Urban
Homesteading Program.   In 1978-79 the average rehabilitation
investment in   the houses was $45,000.   They were   sold to
homesteaders for $1.   The $20,000 average homesteader income
allowed for the cost of rehabilitation.   Housing values have
increased in the area; these same units now sell for $90,000
to $100,000.   Interest rates   for rehabilitation loans were
subsidized   even in   cases where   homesteaders had   adequate
incomes.   None of the local   loan programs imposed maximum-
income limitations, but considered affordability instead.
     A major element   of the program was   the availability of
city-funded,   low-interest rehabilitation loans.   Under the
Rehabilitation Environmental Assistance Loan (REAL) Program,
eligible homeowners   could borrow money   from the city   at 7
percent interest   to rehabilitate   a house.   City staffers
promoted   the   program's   real   estate   tax   advantage.
Rehabilitated urban homesteads were assessed at a level that
reflected the value of residential property in the area, and
was not based on the cost of the rehabilitation.[4]
     The local Urban Homesteading Program guidelines differed
somewhat   from those   of the   federal   Section 810 Program.
Homesteaders had   to satisfy all   fire and safety requirements

within six months after loan settlement and move into the
property.   Within twenty-four months,   all rehabilitation
work had to have been completed and the property certified
as having   met all   applicable   code   standards.   The
homesteader was required to reside in the property for at
least eighteen months, at which time title to the property
was transferred and the property was reassessed.   No
property taxes were due until after the title transfer.

Baltimore attempted to respond to community reactions to
housing programs.   To weather   complaints "that urban
homesteading was not used in the right neighborhoods and did
not serve the right citizens," DHCD implemented the Local
Property Assistance (LPA) Program.[5] Under LPA, homes were
rehabilitated at $50,000 per unit and sold to families with
incomes of less than 80 percent of the SMSA median, that is,
meeting low- and moderate-income criteria.   The city wrote
down the mortgage rate and assisted with financing.   The
houses were located in urban renewal areas around the city
due to requirements attached to the use of block grant
funds.

Section 810 Urban Homesteading Program in Baltimore

In 1975, DHCD initiated the federal Urban Homesteading
Demonstration Program in the community of Park Heights.   In
1978, HUD approved Park Heights for continued participation
in the Section 810 Program, and this operation succeeded the
demonstration.   In the application to HUD for participation,
Park Heights was described as a "new community of people in
an old community of buildings."[6] This description reflected
the rapid population turnover within fifteen years from
moderately affluent Jewish residents to moderate- and low-
income blacks.   The community had most of the problems of a
physically old area but little of the social stability of an
established community.   Park Heights was diverse.   Some
blocks were plagued by serious overcrowding, low income,
transiency, and deteriorating housing.   Others, especially
in the northern and eastern sections, boasted a middle-class
semi-professional population, a high rate of homeownership,
and attractive neighborhoods.[7] Socioeconomically, Park
Heights manifested the larger city's problems in microcosm
with housing quality and costs out of line, insufficient
sanitation and general city services, high unemployment, a
high crime rate, and a poor educational system.   The area
had previously been designated as an urban renewal area,
focusing upon physical rehabilitation and social
redevelopment to salvage the parts that had remained stable.
Urban homesteading was introduced as another means to ensure
the success of ongoing efforts.

An agreement with the Park Heights Community Corporation
(PHCC) gave priority to Park Heights residents who were
renters at that time.   The PHCC, an umbrella group of
residents and other spokespersons for the community,
included business operators among its most active members.
Baltimore's Section 810 application stated that community

involvement was important to the success of the Park Heights renewal plan--of which urban homesteading was a part.

Park Heights became the target area because it contained the most substantial number of vacant buildings owned by HUD in the city. The 83 properties in the program comprised almost half of the city's maximum total HUD inventory of 168 in 1975. The Baltimore Board of Estimates' Authorization was required before submitting applications to HUD. In addition, applications were subject to A-95 review by the State Clearinghouse and the Regional Planning Council. No opposition arose from either agency.

The same staff that ran the local program--the Home Ownership Development Division of the DHCD was responsible for administering the Section 810 Program. The program was implemented through the Division's City-owned Property Management Unit (COPMU). The COPMU homesteading staff was responsible for selecting properties, marketing designated houses, running the application and award process, and the rehabilitation service for estimating, underwriting, and escrow management of loans under the rehabilitation loan programs. A public-conducted lottery was the vehicle for selection among potentially eligible homesteaders. Initially, thirteen full-time positions were established in the Home Ownership Development Division related to the support and administration of both homesteading programs. Other DHCD· divisions and city departments provided on-call services.

Under the Section 810 scenario, estimated rehabilitation costs ranged from $16,500 to $31,500. Baltimore provided financing for homesteaders primarily through the use of the City Housing Assistance Loan Program (CHAP), and a low-interest program with a variable interest rate (1 to 7 percent) depending upon family size and income. Section 312 rehabilitation loans and some state-funded loans were also provided.

Section 810 Urban Homesteading in Detroit

The urban homesteading concept had been considered in Detroit prior to its initial implementation in 1979.[8] The city had been an unsuccessful applicant in the second round of Urban Homesteading Demonstration cities chosen in 1977. In 1979, an application was submitted to HUD for participation in the operating program with the approval of the Detroit city council. The application was subject to A-95 review and was summarily scrutinized by: the South-eastern Michigan Council of Governments (SEMCOG), the Wayne County Planning Commission, the Michigan Department of Civil Rights, and the State Clearinghouse in the Office of Intergovernmental Relations.

There are two urban homesteading areas in Detroit operated under Section 810 guidelines. Area I is on the city's far north side; Area II is on the near west side.

Area I has approximately 92,600 persons, or 7 percent of the city's total population.[9] Since 1970, its population has

declined by about 10 percent.   More   than 50 percent of the
residents   are   members   of   minority   groups--a   significant
change   from 1970,   when approximately   37   percent   of   the
area's population   was minority.   More   than 33   percent of
Area   I   residents have   incomes   below   80 percent   of   the
regional median income.
     The housing stock   declined by 2,020 units   between 1970
and 1979.   Though reasonably sound,   it was forty to fifty
years old and had begun to show signs of deterioration.   The
city   cited   the   presence   of   vacant   HUD   properties   as
detrimental   to   the   area   and   threatening   to   property
values.[10]   Growing   numbers   of   vacant   lots   also   had   a
blighting influence on the community.
     Detroit's Community and   Economic Development Department
(CEDD)   cited three   primary reasons for designating   Area I
for homesteading: the high concentration   of structurally
sound vacant HUD properties; the existence of several active
community organizations;   and the   allocation of other funds
for neighborhood improvement in this area.
     During   the   late   1950s,   Area   II   underwent   rapid
transition when   moderate-income Jewish   residents left   and
lower-income   blacks   replaced them.   The   population   had
stabilized when   urban homesteading   assistance was   sought;
however, serious housing problems remained.   No appreciable
change in   median income or population   composition occurred
between   1970 and   1980,   and   overall population   declined
slightly.
     Most Area   II structures   are single-family   brick homes
built prior to 1930.   Owner-occupancy was very high in 1979,
at   90 percent.   The   general   neighborhood condition   was
stable;   housing ranged from   well-maintained to dilapidated
and open to   trespassers.   However,   it was   felt that with
minimal improvements, the area could be revived.
     The   Urban   Homesteading Program   application noted   that
basic exterior   maintenance had   obviously been   deferred on
the occupied dwellings and was compounded by the presence of
vacant houses.   The application   cited the   involvement of
neighborhood commercial   strips as an   integral part   of the
community development   effort.   The   commercial areas   were
still active but bordering upon unviability.
     Area II was selected for   urban homesteading because of:
(1)   the high quality of housing within the boundaries;   (2)
the high   rate of   owner-occupancy,   which   would presumably
contribute toward the success of the program;   (3)   existing
neighborhood organizations   directed toward   improved living
conditions;   and (4) current city-improvement efforts in the
area.
     Through urban   homesteading and   other programs   in both
Areas I and II, the city hoped to stem the flow of residents
outward.   Other objectives   were to   reclaim good   housing
stock; demolish uninhabitable structures; encourage property
maintenance;   slow down abandonment;   and generally improve
the city's attractiveness.[11]
     Local   operating   rules   and   regulations   to   implement
Section 810 Urban   Homesteading are promulgated by   the CEDD
staff.   A   homesteading advisory board   in each area   is to
provide   input   and   feedback   relative   to   the   program's

success.   Board members are   elected by neighborhood groups
and vary in number.   Detroit urban homestead Manager Russell
White has   indicated that   the northside   board is   inactive
while the westside board meets infrequently.

The program's express   goals are to provide   housing for
low- and moderate-income citizens who   could not afford such
property otherwise   and to mitigate the   blighting influence
of vacant housing.   Participation is restricted to nonowners
of residential property with bona   fide family status.[12] The
staff assigned grew from five professionals and one clerical
assistant   to nine   program professionals   and one   clerical
assistant by 1985   and declined to one   program professional
and one clerical assistant by 1988.

Detroit's CEDD was selective about the properties chosen
for the program.   Criteria   for selection   were structural
soundness,   feasibility of rehabilitation,   and stability of
the block on which it stood.

Applicants were initially screened   to determine whether
they met basic   criteria,   including low to   moderate income
status ($25,000 or less)   and citizenship.   They were then
pre-qualified for   specific housing types based   upon family
size.   Periodic open houses were   held to display available
properties.   Homesteaders were   linked with properties
through a lottery system.

The   estimated   rehabilitation   value   per   property   is
$15,000.   In accordance with the Section 810 guidelines, the
maximum   repair   cost   cannot   exceed $27,000   per   unit.
Targeting the   program to low- and   moderate-income families
imposes constraints on the amount of rehabilitation that can
be   done affordably.   In   addition,   funding sources   are
limited   due   to   the underwriting   standards   of   financial
institutions   as   they   pertain   to   lower-income   families.
Consequently,   Section 312 loans   and some CDBG-funded loans
and grants   are the principal   funding sources   available to
homesteaders through CEDD.   Homesteaders may   also qualify
for   loans through   the Michigan   State Housing   Development
Authority's Community Housing Improvement Program (CHIP).

Pre- and post-ownership counseling   was provided through
a contractual arrangement with   a private,   nonprofit social
service association: the Neighborhood Services Organization.
The   provision   of   counseling   began   in   1984   to   address
problems associated   with first-time   homeownership,   moving
trauma, and high percentages of public-assistance recipients
(80 percent).

Detroit's Local Urban Homesteading Program

In February 1983,   the city instituted its   as-is Urban
Homesteading Program,   a citywide   program using non-Section
810   federal   properties   and   city-held,   tax-reverted
properties.   Implementation did not   require   legislative
action since the authority provided under other programs was
adequate.   To date,   this   approach has   yielded   fewer
properties   than through   Section 810.   The local   program
removes   the   onus   from   city   officials   to   assist   the

homesteader in securing rehabilitation financing or providing financing as included in the Section 810 regulations.   This effort also differs from Section 810 by aiming toward higher income households; hence, there are no maximum income limitations.

This approach offers two advantages over Section 810. First, the houses are available in a wider range of neighborhoods where conditions make them unsuitable for Section 810 designation.   Second, the program can be used for spot revitalization to salvage isolated instances of vacant housing.   This may be a realistic alternative to large-scale revitalization of entire neighborhoods.   The city pays between $6,000 and $15,000 to acquire HUD properties for use in this program.   Property selection is based upon location as related to marketability, bankability, feasibility of rehabilitation, and price.   The rehabilitation costs for properties in this local program are estimated to be between $8,000 and $12,000. Homesteaders are allowed six months to meet minimum health and safety standards and obtain an occupancy permit; an additional six months is allowed to complete the balance of the rehabilitation.   The properties must be occupied for at least five years.   Homesteaders are not offered tax abatements or any form of tax relief.   While held by the city, all urban homesteading properties are exempt from property taxes.   Some homesteaders who acquire property during an exempt period benefit fortuitously by not paying taxes for the period in effect.

In 1983, the city council passed a Nuisance Abatement Ordinance.   Patterned after a similar ordinance in Philadelphia, this legislation would allow nuisance abaters to identify abandoned properties, abate the nuisance (rehabilitate them), and reside there for an unspecified period.   The occupant could obtain title to the property if, and when, it reverted to the city.   If the owner attempted to reclaim the property, the occupant was to recover all funds spent to rehabilitate it.   The Nuisance Abatement Ordinance was not immediately implemented by city departments; the mayor's office and the law department maintained that it was unconstitutional.

The Association of Community Organizations for Reform Now (ACORN) has been instrumental in promoting the cause of nuisance abaters--also known as squatters--in Detroit.   This network of organizations has been involved across the country, aiding other groups concerned with homeownership for the poor.   ACORN has also provided assistance and legal support to homesteaders on an individual basis.   The organization was the plaintiff in the lawsuit over implementation of Detroit's Nuisance Abatement Ordinance.

In November 1987, the Wayne County Circuit Court ruled favorably for the implementation of the Nuisance Abatement Ordinance.   The city began to operate the program in February 1988 through the Department of Buildings and Safety Engineering.   No funds were made available to aid the nuisance abaters although eligible persons could avail themselves of programs offered through the CEDD.

Conceptually, abaters should receive title to the properties
through a quiet title process in which the city can petition
through circuit court for title to the properties based upon
their abandonment and nuisance to the community.   There is
some doubt that this is a legal process.   The propriety will
be determined in court if, and when, challenges to the
city's authority arise.

Philadelphia's Local Urban Homesteading Program

By the late 1960s, Philadelphia had seen the effects of
suburbanization, assimilation, racial and ethnic invasions,
and confrontations in housing abandonment.   In 1968
Councilman Joseph E. Coleman initially suggested urban
homesteading as a possible way to remedy these problems.[13]
The city ultimately adopted its local homesteading ordinance
in July 1973 and the first homesteads were awarded in June
1974.   Areas included in the local Urban Homesteading
Program were individual blocks approved by the city council
in the following neighborhoods: North Philadelphia, West
Philadelphia, Northwest Philadelphia, Germantown, Southwest
Philadelphia, and Logan.

Under the enabling legislation, Ordinance 543, the mayor
appointed an Urban Homesteading Board.   The board was
comprised eleven persons, representing the following groups:
architects, contractors, the Buildings Trade Council, the
clergy, representatives of savings and loans institutions,
the general public, and two city council members.   Three
city officials served as ex-officio members: deputy managing
director of housing, executive director of the redevelopment
authority, and the executive director of the Philadelphia
city planning commission.   The Board was empowered to
operate outside the formal structure of local government to
recommend foreclosure proceedings to secure vacant
properties; to secure adequate financing for the
homesteader; and to establish local councils to promote
homesteading in their respective areas.   A technical staff
of twelve conducted program operations.

The incipient Urban Homesteading Program's goals were:
(1) to return vacant properties to the tax rolls; (2) to
place people in homes who wanted to be homeowners but were
unable to do so in the normal market; and (3) to use
homesteading as a first effort toward devising more
sophisticated approaches for dealing with abandoned
housing.[14]

The fact that Councilman Coleman introduced urban
homesteading may account for its lack of mayoral support.
In contrast to Baltimore, where the mayor assumed an
activist role in implementing homesteading and was publicly
associated with it, the Philadelphia mayor's office was
accused of obstructionism and attempts to thwart the
program.   The original allocation of $1.5 million for
mortgage guarantees was delayed, as was the disbursement of
funds to fill staff positions.   The Pennsylvania Housing
Finance Agency and private foundations supplied initial

mortgage financing. Administrative posturing made urban homesteading dependent on a number of external parties, slowing its output.[15]

In 1974, it was estimated that the number of abandoned residential units totaled 24,000--only 250 of which were controlled by the city. The city had been reluctant to assume ownership of worthless parcels, hoping that owners might regain interest in them if foreclosure was delayed. Of the 250 city-owned structures, only 8 were deemed suitable for homesteading; extensive deterioration had occurred during periods of vacancy. The Pennsylvania state legislature later passed a special fast-take law that enabled the city to take title in six months--although in reality, the process still took nine months to a year.

Early in the program's operation, city officials identified HUD properties as particularly suitable targets for urban homesteading. At that time, HUD owned just over 3,000 units, obtained through mortgage foreclosure, that had experienced only slight deterioration. The city purchased properties directly from HUD for early rounds of conveyance at an average cost of $500.[16]

The Philadelphia Housing Development Corporation (PHDC) played a role even in this first homesteading effort. PHDC was to hold title to properties awaiting conveyance to homesteaders, since the urban homesteading board was not legally empowered to do so. Gift properties, donated by owners in exchange for absolution from delinquent taxes, provided another housing source for this venture. HUD's PROP did not provide suitable properties for homesteading: most were badly deteriorated--among the worst in the HUD inventory--and none were accepted. This problem, coupled with the existence of more suitable HUD properties, may have contributed to Philadelphia's leading role in the passage of federal Section 810 legislation. Councilman Coleman prepared reports and testified before Congress, encouraging the legislation and federal support of the program.

Local guidelines required homesteaders (1) to begin rehabilitation no later than sixty days after title was acquired; (2) to complete the rehabilitation within two years; and (3) to live in the structures at least five years. The program sought individuals who, beyond meeting formal requirements, had proven construction skills or other ability to undertake sweat equity.

Financing arrangements involved a two-tiered process during the period when city funds were withheld. A consortium of churches, volunteers, and financiers contributed to a $300,000 loan fund--The Urban Homesteading Finance Corporation. Homesteaders received small start-up loans to begin reconstruction and start establishing equity in their homes. The loans were typically for six months at 6 percent interest. The Pennsylvania Housing Finance Agency provided long-term mortgage financing at variable interest rates ranging from 3 to 7 percent for terms of five to fifteen years. Homesteaders enjoyed substantial savings when compared with conventional borrowers with market-rate mortgage loans of 12 percent. While this two-part process emerged out of necessity, it did partially resolve the

difficulty of making a long-term financial commitment before
building equity through property rehabilitation.

Section 810 Urban Homesteading in Philadelphia

In February 1975, the Philadelphia city council enacted
legislation that authorized the city to participate in the
Section 810 Urban Homesteading Demonstration Program.
Specific blocks in the Germantown and Winfield neighborhoods
were designated. Until 1978, the Section 810 demonstration
functioned independently of the city administration, under
the auspices of the Urban Homesteading Board.   In addition
to the program's suspension in 1978, other problems included
delinquest loans, dissatisfaction with repair work, shoddy
workmanship, unprocessed applications, and poor materials.[17]
In spite of these difficulties, all 362 properties in this
program were homesteaded.   As the city's OHCD assumed
control of the program, it aimed to make it smaller and more
concentrated.   The Urban Homesteading Board dissolved when
the program became a city function.[18] Philadelphia did not
apply for participation in the Section 810 operating program
until 1982--approximately four years after it began.   The
approved program was ultimately turned over to the PHDC.
     The city of Philadelphia designated one neighborhood,
Southwest Philadelphia, for the Section 810 Operating
Program that began in 1982. Another neighborhood, Overbrook
was added in 1986. Prior to urban homesteading, Southwest
had never been part of any federally assisted program.   The
program aimed to serve only low- and moderate-income
persons, and the area was chosen for its strengths as well
as weaknesses. Southwest Philadelphia is predominantly an
area of owner-occupants: more than 70 percent of the
residents owned their own homes in 1970.   The area has a
strong public transportation system.   In 1970, about 45
percent of the workers used public transit to get to work.[19]
The Southwest black population increased dramatically
between 1970 and 1980, from 31 percent to 75 percent.   A
rapid turnover in housing stock resulted, and the community
atmosphere was somewhat destabilized.
     In 1980, Southwest had 13,292 housing units and a 10.2
percent vacancy rate.   All urban homesteading properties in
this community are brick row houses.   The program
application submitted to HUD states that the median real
estate prices in the area are comparatively low, close to
$10,000 per house versus $17,500 for the entire city.
Prices are lowest in the northeast section of the program
area, which is nearest to Bartram Village, a 500-unit public
housing project in need of substantial repair.[20]
     When it was chosen as the urban homesteading site,
Philadelphia officials described the Southwest area as being
in the early stages of decline.   At that time, according to
the city's Department of License and Inspection, the area
had a 5.2 percent vacancy rate.   Over 75 percent of the
long-term vacant residential single-family structures were
in good structural condition and required a lower degree of
rehabilitation than average. As such, the city deemed these

properties particularly amenable to rehabilitation funded through home-improvement loans, sweat equity, or low-cost public rehabilitation.

Variable-rate loans for rehabilitation are provided through the Neighborhood Housing Services (NHS) Program targeted in the same area. The NHS loan fund consists of grants from foundations, the Neighborhood Reinvestment Corporation (the national coordinator for NHS programs), and the city of Philadelphia. A limited number of Section 312 loans are available. Homesteaders may also seek loans through the Action Loan Program at interest rates of 3 to 4 percent. In keeping with the HUD edict requiring a coordinated neighborhood improvement plan, commercial revitalization and capital improvements are slated: these include low-interest business loans and construction of a new gymnasium. In addition to the area's Gift Property Program, the OHCD contracted with a nonprofit group to rehabilitate and sell vacant properties at below-market sales prices to low- and moderate-income families.

The urban homesteading program was expanded to Overbrook in an effort to target a higher-income community. It is an area with fewer vacant HUD-held and other properties. Project officials sought two objectives in selecting this area, a more diverse economic mix and greater impact. The median family income in 1980 was $14,231 slightly lower than the city median of $16,388. Between 1970 and 1980 the proportion of black population rose from 62% to 94%. The population change in Overbrook and Southwest was similar, but the housing values differed markedly. Overbrook property values averaged $17,800 in Overbrook compared to $11,005 for Southwest. The vacancy rate in Overbrook increased significantly from 1970-80 from three percent to eight percent. These is similar to the overall city increase from 4.6% to 9.5%.

The new blocks in Overbrook were contiguous to the original area. It was felt that the additional properties located there would complement the initial activities in Southwest. Another factor considered was the decreasing number of HUD-owned structures available in the first site. Without additional properties, the city was faced with the possibility of unused Section 810 funds. Southwest had also been designated for the Philadelphia NHS Program and was in high demand by persons seeking affordable single-family homes.

The original staff assigned to administer the Urban Homesteading Program under the independent board included thirteen full-time and two part-time employees. The size of the staff under PHDC was reduced to two full-time and six part-time employees.

The maximum allowable rehabilitation cost corresponds with the maximum loan available through the Section 312 Program, $27,000. The maximum acquisition cost is also in line with Section 312 guidelines, pegged at $15,000. PHDC also provides an eight-week training course in which homesteaders can learn to make certain repairs that do not require a contractor.

COMPARISONS OF PROGRAM OUTPUT

The quantitative output of the Urban Homesteading Program is one indicator of goal attainment. The data available on the program are instructive in two respects: to compare overall results among the three cities, and to compare outputs of local city programs with the Section 810 Program. (See Table 6.2 for urban homesteading property production for the various programs.)

Baltimore. The record of urban homestead production in Baltimore compares favorably with the other two cities. The local (626) rather than the federal (70) program offered the overwhelming majority of these homesteads. As previously noted, the vast majority of vacant properties in Baltimore were city-owned in contrast to Detroit and Philadelphia, where HUD held a sizable proportion. The local program is essentially complete with all properties at least conditionally transferred to homesteaders. The local program's function as a part of the community development/housing strategy was fulfilled. Three cases are involved in litigation related to the terms of the homesteading agreement.

The Baltimore Area HUD office and the Baltimore OHCD agreed to close out the federal program in Park Heights January 1984. As late as February 1983, the HUD area office had generally approved of performance under the Section 810 Program and the steps taken to resolve problem cases. The HUD area office initiated the close-out in December 1983 when overall departmental performance and management were evaluated in relation to length of the program (7 1/2 years at the time), current neighborhood characteristics, and recent trends. The three reasons in support of the close-out were: the lack of suitable properties; unacceptable administrative capacity; and current conditions that affect the program's feasibility and cost-effectiveness. The scarcity of vacant HUD properties in the area accounts for the small number of properties in the program. Only three properties were taken for homesteading between 1981 and 1983. By 1985, HUD had only seventy-one vacant properties throughout Baltimore. The properties were not suitably aggregated for designation as an urban homesteading target area.

Conveyance problems occurred for various reasons. Some properties were re-homesteaded one or more times; others had become delinquent in loan payments; some are involved in litigation related to the terms of the homesteading agreement. Eight properties were found to be too expensive to rehabilitate, and alternative uses such as demolition and alternative marketing are being sought.[21] A HUD monitoring document indicates that five of these properties were never homesteaded. In addition, the Baltimore HUD Office found that the program-management structure of the Baltimore DHCD did not comply with new implementation requirements that

Table 6.2
Urban Homesteading Program Statistics

Program Description	Source of Homesteading Properties					Properties transferred Locality to homesteader (Conditional Conveyance)	Properties transferred Locality to homesteader (Final Conveyance)
	HUD Section 810	HUD Other	Other Federal	Local	Total		
Baltimore (federal program)[1]	81	0	0	2	83	83	75
Baltimore (local program)[2]	0	0	0	626	626	626	623
Detroit (federal program)[3]	190	85	9	76	360	256	0
Detroit (local program)[4]	0	40	0	13	53	13	165[5]
Philadelphia (local program)[2]	N/A	N/A	N/A	N/A	267	267	267
Philadelphia (federal program)[1]	553	27	20	38	600	550	234

[1] As of September 1987

[2] As of December 1984

[3] As of September 1985

[4] As of November 1984

[5] As of April 1988

became   effective   in   fiscal   1984.   The   expense   of
restructuring the administrative organization would not be
cost-effective or feasible given the overall status of the
project and the lack of suitable homesteading properties.

Market conditions were blamed for creating changes in
the Park Heights community that affected the achievement of
objectives   and   the   feasibility   of   future   program
implementation.   Homesteaders able to meet the estimated
costs of repairs were difficult to attract to the area, and
funds were not available to market the properties under a
governmental effort.

Detroit.   The city that had the country's largest inventory
of vacant HUD houses (16,000 in 1975), has a comparatively
small program. (See Table 6.3.)   Just 179 properties have
been transferred from HUD to the city since 1979, and 137 of
those have been conditionally conveyed to homesteaders. The
local HUD inventory had dropped to 577 by 1985. This is
consistent with the national trend of drastic reduction in
HUD-owned property inventory (from a high point of 75,000 at
the end of 1974 to 16,304 by the end of fiscal 1983). HUD
does gain properties each year, such as the 27,772 acquired
in fiscal 1983, some of which are potentially available for
homesteading. The overall HUD inventory, however, has
declined due to increased sales. The transfer of HUD
properties to local homesteading programs has accounted for
less than 3 percent of all HUD properties disposed of since
1975.

The output of Detroit's Section 810 Program was affected
by the decision to focus on low- and moderate-income
households. This approach restricts rehabilitation funding
available, particularly from private sources; most lower-
income homesteaders are solely reliant upon a limited amount
of federal dollars. Furthermore, the target population's
financial limitations render higher-cost houses unfeasible
for the program. The CEDD seemed very careful not to
acquire properties that were badly deteriorated and could
yield an unusable parcel. The lack of progress is strongly
linked to limited resources. Final conveyance of the
properties to homesteaders has been processed slowly. City
officials estimate that while over 100 properties are
eligible for final transfer to homesteaders, only 16 had
been processed in early 1988.

The Section 810 Program has come to a virtual
standstill. Detroit has not taken any new applications from
prospective homesteaders since 1984. No Section 810
properties have been requested through HUD since 1985.
Those parcels remaining in the city's inventory are being
considered for alternative use in keeping with HUD
guidelines. Possible uses included demolition and rental
for low-income persons. The former option is a possibility
for buildings exhibiting serious deterioration since
acquisition from HUD. In the latter instance, private
investors will renovate the structures and rent them to
eligible households.

Table 6.3
Vacant HUD Single-Family Properties

City	Maximum HUD Properties	1985 HUD Properties	1988 HUD Properties	HUD Properties Conveyed for Section 810
Baltimore	167[1]	71	151	81
Detroit	16,674[2]	466	948	275
Philadelphia	4,592[3]	412	1,060	580

[1]September 1974

[2]February 1975

[3]May 1975

In 1986, the HUD area office conducted a monitoring review to measure compliance with program guidelines. The major concern cited was inactivity since 199 properties had not been conveyed to homesteaders. HUD proposed the consideration of alternative uses for 46 of those structures which were not suitable for the program. Among the possible alternative uses is demolition in those cases where extreme deterioration has occurred. Some of the properties had been in the city program since 1981 and had been repeatedly vandalized and open to trespass.

The likelihood of program termination is great in Detroit. HUD has been slow to enforce close-out of the program in spite of policies that would permit such an action. Communities that do not meet an established threshold of five properties per year for two consecutive years are generally moved toward close-out. Politically, with the popularity of the Nuisance Abatement Ordinance that authorizes squatting under city guidelines, ending the Section 810 Program would be highly criticized. Without the

attention of the media or organized investigation, Section
810 may fade into obscurity.
    In another   effort,   the city's version   of urban
homesteading--the as-is program--has involved a total of
fifty-three properties.   At the first lottery in August
1983,   fifty properties were matched with homesteaders
required to secure their own financing.   Ultimately, thirty-
two of the applicants could not obtain financing and/or
misunderstood   the program's intent.   The   thirty-two
properties were recycled into the second, and last, lottery
drawing in November 1984.   The final dispositions of the
latest homesteaders is not yet determined.   The locations of
the   properties   are   predominantly   in   more   stable
neighborhoods of   northwest and   northeast Detroit.   These
areas seemed likely to attract residents who are eligible
for conventional   rehabilitation   financing.   By 1988,
however, this program was also inactive--the victim of its
own design.   Homesteaders selected under this process were
frequently unable to complete the process.   A further
demonstration of the city's difficulty in implementing the
urban homesteading concept is its decision to terminate the
as-is program.

Philadelphia.   Numerically, Philadelphia is the most
productive urban homesteading city studied.   In the locally
legislated program, 267 properties were homesteaded.   The
Section 810 Demonstration Program figures are encouraging in
that all 362 properties had at least been conveyed to
homesteaders.   The current Section 810 operating program,
beset by two suspensions,   conditionally transferred an
impressive 104 properties between July 1984 and December
1984.   The program director, at that time, who had held the
position less than a year,   expressed an inclination toward
high productivity and expected to expand the program area
boundaries.   In 1988,   two additional neighborhoods with a
substantial quantity of HUD-held properties had been
identified.   The areas, with HUD approval, may be added to
the Section 810 Program.
    The proram suspension in 1978 led its revamping under
the auspices of the city's OHCD and transferral to the PHDC.
There were delays in program operations during this process.
Partially as a result of this problem, Philadelphia was not
positioned to submit an application for the Section 810
operating program until 1980, although it was enacted in
1978 and the city had participated in the demonstration that
had begun in 1974.
    Philadelphia's OHCD makes significant use of nonprofit
organizations in carrying out community- and economic-
development activities.   Therefore, contracting with PHDC to
run the Urban Homesteading Program was consistent with past
practices.   At the time, PHDC had already assumed all
housing rehabilitation programs and had been charged to
address the housing needs of low- and moderate-income
households.   The program assumed the characteristics of
PHDC, which gives production high priority.   In the case of

Section 810, this occurred at the expense of program guidelines and resulted in the second suspension in 1982. HUD area office monitoring found that properties were not being conveyed in as-is condition (no repairs) as mandated. CDBG and foundation funds had been utilized to complete partial rehabilitation to make the properties economically feasible to the target low- and moderate-income population before conveyance. PHDC justified the action based upon the poor condition of the structures and the attendant repair costs to be borne by the homesteader. The program was reinstated only after PHDC and the city agreed to adhere to federal regulations.

Comparison of Local and Federal Programs

This section will question the extent of local discretion in Section 810 homesteading--how much was actually available and how it was utilized. The degree to which federal guidelines can realistically address local circumstances is hampered by their broad application. Because Section 810 resulted from compromise among legislators and administrators, it was unlikely that they would reflect the preferences of any one locality. Comparing local and federal homesteading programs is helpful in determining the adequacy of federal criteria. The local urban homesteading programs, free of federal influence, approximate quasi-experimental controls. Theoretically, local guidelines will more absolutely reflect local conditions (to the extent that the program is free from federal influence from funding, for example). A comparison can identify local program preferences that are at odds with federal provisions. Local preferences are expressed through local political agents and are not necessarily unanimous.

Participation in Section 810 Urban Homesteading was not mandatory, but if adopted, program guidelines applied unilaterally: (1) a coordinated approach toward neighborhood improvement and the prohibition of scattered site improvements; (2) the meeting of applicable local standards for decent, safe, and sanitary housing within eighteen months after occupancy; and (3) continued occupancy for at least three consecutive years from the initial occupancy date.[22] Local program guidelines suggest that federal criteria did not address area needs. The divergent points are briefly described here.

First, all three cities adopted scattered site approaches to homesteading in their local programs. This was seemingly more compatible with local needs and political pressures. The first program in Baltimore, Stirling Street, consisted of a block of forty-two properties technically considered a scattered site, not a neighborhood, project. Most of Baltimore's locally homesteaded properties were situated throughout the city. Philadelphia's local homesteads were similarly dispersed in several neighborhoods. Detroit's local program, developed after the adoption of Section 810, was directed toward vacant

(predominantly   HUD-owned)   properties   throughout   the
northwest and northeast sections of the city.
    Second,   cities   enforced   residency   requirements
consistent with their target population goals.   The original
Baltimore program allowed six months to complete structural
repairs and twenty-four months to meet local housing codes.
An occupancy period of twenty-four months was required.
Baltimore's shorter required residency period supports the
thrust to attract upper-income persons by both reducing
their risk somewhat (two years' required occupancy)   and
allowing for quicker turnover and the possibility of capital
gain.   Capital gain has been an incentive for middle-income
home buyers.
    Both   Philadelphia   and   Detroit   local   guidelines
emphasized the homeownership aspect.   Longer periods of
residency discourage speculation.   Philadelphia's initial
program provided twenty-four months to meet local building
codes and required five years of residency.   The increased
time for repairs enables sweat equity by low-income persons.
The newer Detroit program allows six months to meet minimum
health and safety standards,   one year to complete all
rehabilitation work, and requires a five-year occupancy
period.   Less rehabilitation time may actually be required
on the houses acquired for Detroit's local effort because
they are in better condition.   The shorter time reduces the
feasibility of sweat equity, which can take more time to
yield the same quality of work.[23] Yet, the term of residence
confirms that the emphasis is homeownership and not
investment.   The deviations between cities and the federal
government are not great, but suggest that federal
guidelines cannot easily reach consonance with all cities.
    For unique reasons, each Section 810 city experience
difficulty in implementing the program despite the
discretion allowed. Baltimore's eligible properties did not
meet the location requirement for targeting and was short-
lived.   The condition of Detroit's housing stock was not
suitable for rehabilitation by the low- and moderate-income
target population;   the areas chosen met targeting and
coordination mandates but did not appeal to upper-income
groups.   The program in Detroit has been short-circuited.
The Philadelphia program's difficulties are most apparent in
the actual and threatened suspensions.   Ironically, the
numerical success in urban homesteading is due, in part, to
a program implementer's daring action to circumvent
guidelines.   The cities proceeded, nonetheless, with their
programs subject to these and other key influences.   The
major factors that affected implementation are recounted and
described in the next chapter.

NOTES

    1.   James W. Hughes and Kenneth D. Bleakley, Jr., Urban
Homesteading (New Brunswick, New Jersey: The Center for
Urban Policy Research, Rutgers University, 1975), p. 68.
    2.   Ibid., p. 91.
    3.   Interview with Thomas Jaudon, Baltimore Department

of Housing and Community Development, November 28, 1984.

4. Baltimore Department of Housing and Community
Development, Homesteading -- The Second Year: 1975,   1976,
p. 5.

5. Interview with Ellsworth Andrews, HUD, Baltimore
Area Office, November 28, 1984.

6. Baltimore Urban Homesteading application,   August
27, 1975, p. 17.

7. Ibid., p. 18.

8. Mark Van Allsburg, "Property Abandonment in
Detroit," Wayne Law Review 20 (March 1974), 881.

9. Detroit Urban Homesteading application,   June 20,
1979, p. 3.

10. Ibid.

11. Ibid.

12. Family is defined as "two or more persons living
together"; marriage is not required.

13. Hughes and Bleakley, Urban Homesteading, p. 133.

14. Ibid., p. 141.

15. Ibid., p. 149.

16. Ibid., p. 138.

17. Interview with Julia Robinson, Philadelphia Office
of Housing, November 15, 1984.

18. Interview with Vincent Coles, Philadelphia Housing
Development Corporation, November 15, 1984.

19. Philadelphia Urban Homesteading application, p. 4.

20. Ibid.

21. Telephone interview with Alan Gee on May 20, 1985.

22. The 1983 Housing Act changed the time lines to
require conformance with local housing standards within
three years and continued occupancy for at least 5 years.

23. Sumka, "Urban Homesteading," HUD, Washington, D.C.,
1981 (unpublished report), p. 6.

7

Elements of Program Variation

The information gathered on the operation of Urban Homesteading Programs can be compared from four major perspectives: administration and operation, including agency characteristics; financial and political support at the local level; the thrust of local goals--specifically as related to those who benefit; and the influence of federal input.

PROGRAM OPERATION AND ADMINISTRATION

Because the Section 810 Program did not provide administrative funds, implementing agencies had to redirect existing organizational resources to run it. Unique patterns of mutual adaptation between program directives and the cities emerged.

The characteristics of participating agencies influenced the implementation of Urban Homesteading Programs. Berman has found that implementation deliverers, while translating the adopted project or plan into an operational reality, repeatedly choose to adapt project plans to their standard behavior or to adapt their behavior to suit the plan. Implementation, he concluded, can follow one of four paths: non-implementation: no adaptation in the project plan or in deliverer behavior; cooperation: no adaptation in deliverer behavior, but adaptation in the project to accommodate existing routines; technological learning: no adaptation of the project plan but adaptation of routinized behavior to accommodate the plan; or mutual adaptation: adaptation of both the project and deliverer behavior.[1] The three subject cities--in varying degrees--demonstrated the fourth mode of behavior.

Baltimore is conventionally considered a pioneer in housing and community development. The administrative mechanism of Baltimore's urban homesteading effort has been the most consistent of the three cities. Baltimore appeared to be best prepared organizationally to run an urban homesteading program. The consolidation of housing functions within the DHCD seemed to minimize the need for external cooperation and support.   In addition,   the local program was already under way at the time   of Section 810's adoption,   suggesting a high degree of consonance with local priorities.   The city thus had an edge in start-up time over programs such as Detroit, which did not have a prior effort, and over Philadelphia, which was undergoing transition.

Few adjustments of staff   assignments were   required to implement the Baltimore program.   At the suggestion of the HUD area office,   a homesteading manager position was established in 1979.   Occasional staffing changes occurred in response to activity levels and the volume of properties handled.

To the extent that the Section 810 Program guidelines encumbered local preferences,   they were too restrictive for large-scale   adoption   or   institutionalization.   The neighborhood targeting requirement was at variance with the scattered site approach promoted   in Baltimore's local program to achieve community development/housing goals.   As Berman found, rather than becoming a routinized part of the delivery system, a project might fade away, "especially when the macro-policy that precipitated local adoption is no longer an idea in good currency."[2] Close-out of the program may indicate, among other things, a lack of dependence upon HUD for assistance.   DHCD was much more successful in conducting its local program.

Although Detroit's program also operated in a city agency,   Section 810 did necessitate the establishment of a new Urban Homesteading Unit for that purpose.   The staff size grew as activity levels and work load increased and shrunk as they declined.   Detroit proceeded cautiously with urban homesteading implementation.   This approach may be a result of adverse impacts of previous programs as well as HUD criticism about other rehabilitation efforts.   CEDD's inclination   toward   contractor   repairs   and   periodic inspections--rather than sweat equity--allowed the agency to maintain a greater degree of control and accountability.

The Detroit HUD area office, in a monitoring letter dated April 19, 1985, stated that the shared roles of CEDD and the Buildings and Safety Engineering Department for rehabilitation inspection was a cause of program delay.   Responsibility for housing matters, as mentioned in Chapter 5, was fragmented and overlapped with other city departments. Lack of direct control over essential functions hampered departmental progress.

In 1983,   HUD issued a monitoring report on Detroit's total CDBG program, criticizing its overall rehabilitation effort.   Low productivity and high administration to production ratios were cited.   A national HUD official has speculated that a city operates all its rehabilitation programs comparably.[3] If this is the case, the same factors that contributed generally to high administrative and rehabilitation costs per structure may apply to urban homesteading as well.   It is clear that the city did not deem urban homesteading worthy of resource allocation to operate on a more effective scale.   By 1988, efforts had begun in earnest to close out the program with a full-time

staff of one person.   In addition, without the resources of
Baltimore or the orgazational capacity of Philadelphia to
support low to moderate homeownership, Detroit's efforts
were likely to suffer.
The dissenting actions of the two nonprofit agencies
involved in Philadelphia's Section 810 Program could earn it
the title of maverick.   Downs noted the propensity of
implementers to modify the rules: "When empowered to make
choices rational officials will use it to achieve their
goals."[4] Rather than willingly adopting program guidelines,
PHDC attempted to adapt the program to its objectives--by
conveying properties to homeowners in repaired rather than
as-is, condition as mandated.   In the past, HUD's punitive
actions have been successful in achieving compliance; and
PHDC and the city of Philadelphia have responded by adhering
to regulations.   The relative benefit of Section 810 to
Philadelphia apparently exceeds the costs.
Philadelphia's placement of urban homesteading under the
aegis of a nonprofit organization removed it from direct
city control.   Mayor Rizzo's opposition to the first program
may have been partially due to this.   Later, PHDC--as a
noncity entity--was in a position to take risks as the urban
homesteading agency.   Until the legislative changes of 1984,
only the applicant unit of government had to sign the urban
homesteading agreement with HUD.   Therefore, PHDC was not
legally bound by the regulations.   Under the new
requirements, any legally separate and independent agency
(such as PHDC) designated by the applicant to administer the
program had to be an additional party to the agreement.
Joint execution of the agreement was intended to facilitate
its enforcement by HUD, if necessary.   In 1984, HUD also
took action to interpose the city of Philadelphia as a
monitor of PHDC.   The ambiguity of this relationship is
apparent in that city officials hold seats on the PHDC board
of directors.   Downs' discussion of "monitoring the monitor"
reveals that it greatly complicates the power relationship;
there is no easy, satisfactory conclusion.[5] Monitoring and
joint execution of the agreement may reduce PHDC's autonomy.
Whatever program or administrative benefits that may have
accrued through PHDC's operation outside the city structure
may be eliminated as these two processes forge program
accountability.
The placement of Baltimore and Detroit programs within
city line departments, with many other activities and
diverse goals, has required them to compete for funds and
attention.   However, they were less likely to be involved in
an adversarial relationship such as that between the
original urban homesteading board in Philadelphia (an
independent body) and the mayor's office.   Quasi-public
organizations are intended to bypass city bureaucratic
procedures.   However, routine city controls might have
prevented the actions that led to the suspensions in
Philadelphia.   As the federal government imposes more
regulations, the distinctions in the behavior of
implementing agencies may be blurred.

PROGRAM SUPPORT: FINANCIAL

The CDBG is the primary funding source of all three
agencies running the Section 810 Urban Homesteading and
local homesteading programs. Not surprisingly, the flexible
CDBG funds are used for administering urban homesteading as
well as for rehabilitation loans in all three cities.
Detroit was the only city that also provided grants for
homesteading repairs from CDBG funds.   Section 312 loans
were used for rehabilitation in all three cities. Baltimore
was able to leverage CDBG funds with private lender
financing during rehabilitation. Philadelphia had access to
foundation financing for rehabilitation activities.
Unfortunately, the CDBG Grantee Performance Report does not
require communities to report specifically what they have
spent on urban homesteading administration;   therefore,
systematic administrative cost data are unavailable.[6]
Generally, Detroit has enjoyed less success than
Baltimore and Philadelphia in garnering private support for
housing rehabilitation projects.   Cooperation between the
city and local financial institutions has been a perpetual
problem.   Since the Section 235 Program mishaps, the city's
community development agency has been forced to deal with a
particularly complicated housing situation with no clear
solutions.   Commercial bank loans have been secured for
participants in Detroit's as-is program, but not in the
Section 810 effort.   The higher incomes and bankability of
participants in the former program accounts for the
difference.
Limited sweat equity (less than 25 percent of the
repairs) has typically been a part of the urban homesteading
rehabilitation effort in Detroit.   Extensive sweat equity
(up to and exceeding 25 percent) has been a component of the
Philadelphia rehabilitation package.   Emphasis upon self-
help has been promoted through repair workshops that
homesteaders are required to attend.   Baltimore did not
include sweat equity as a part of its rehabilitation of
Section 810 properties, though in some cases substantial
amounts occurred in the local program.
Uncertainty about future funding for federal programs is
endemic: political and procedural processes such as
congressional debate and budget revisions ensure this.   For
urban homesteading, the issue is exacerbated by its
dependence upon other funding sources for administrative and
rehabilitation functions. The two primary sources, CDBG and
Section 312, have been subject to their own adjustments.   In
the case of Section 312, no new allocations have been made
since 1980, hence, and its long-term prospects are doubtful.
Annual CDBG allocations have been reduced.   HUD is required
to review the performance of each local homesteading agency
annually to determine whether it complies with applicable
laws and regulations; whether it has substantially carried
out the program as approved; and whether the agency has the
continuing capacity to carry out the approved program in a
timely manner.   (Performance monitoring may be a part of
this process.) 'Program support and continuation is

contingent upon these findings.   The two-year period in
which funding was withheld from urban homesteading is
testimony to funding aberrations.   Faced with uncertain
prospects, implementers may avoid institutionalization of
programs.

PROGRAM SUPPORT: POLITICAL

In the study of the federal aid process in Oakland,
California,   the connection between federal program outcomes
and local political support was found to be strong.[7] The
extent of political support received varied among urban
homesteading cities.   Baltimore and Philadelphia experienced
varying degrees of support from local political and/or
public officials for their programs.   The impetus to
initiate neighborhood reclamation in Baltimore came from
Robert Embry, Jr.,   first commissioner of the DHCD.   Two
mayors--Schaefer   and   D'Alessandro   III--supported   his
policies and gave him the freedom and authority to pursue a
variety of   innovative   programs,   including   urban
homesteading.   Embry left Baltimore to become HUD Assistant
Secretary for Community Planning and Development (CPD),
where he was credited with continued federal support of
Section 810 and the introduction of the UDAG Program.[8] His
allegiance to Baltimore reportedly continued during his
tenure at HUD.   M. J. Brodie, his successor at DHCD, was
another ardent supporter of urban homesteading.[9]
Councilman Joseph Coleman was an early promoter of
Philadelphia's Urban Homesteading Program and a strong
advocate of federal involvement; his efforts resulted in the
passage of Section 810 Urban Homesteading.   Coleman's close
association with the program contributed to his conflict
with Mayor Rizzo.   He served on the original Urban
Homesteading Board until it was dissolved and the program
was absorbed by the city administration.   The downfall of
the program director in 1978 caused him political
embarrassment.[10] Housing advocates have also had support in
the city council from John Street, who comes from an
activist tradition.[11] Representing a poor, predominantly
black area of North Philadelphia, he has been an advocate
for the housing needs of the urban poor and is largely
responsible for   the Nuisance Abatement   Program (also
referred to as the squatters' ordinance), a variation on the
urban homesteading theme.   The support of two politically
astute   individuals was   instrumental   to   the   initial
implementation of urban homesteading in both Baltimore and
Philadelphia.
Detroit's programs have not enjoyed similar political
support.   Section 810 was adopted largely as the result of
administrative initiative--although the local program was
enacted, in part, as a response to local demands for a
citywide endeavor.   Housing advocates do not enjoy a strong,
consistent voice within or outside city government.   The
urban homesteading constituency, as such, may be embodied in
supporters of the Nuisance Abatement Ordinance made up of

ACORN members and followers. City departments have maintained the position of the mayor relative to the nonimplementation of the ordinance. Prospects for the implementation of the program are viewed with skepticism by officials who doubt its feasibility. The various housing-oriented, community-based organizations are virtual competitors for limited CDBG funds.

ACHIEVEMENT OF LOCAL GOALS

The flexibility of Section 810 guidelines permits localities to develop and pursue their own goals. HUD also allowed discretion to cities in carrying out the requisite functions entailed in the urban homesteading process: selection of neighborhoods, properties, and homesteaders; conditional conveyance; and arrangement of financing. Each city did indeed perform these functions uniquely; however, no significant variation in effect was observed. The significant discretion was afforded in determining program goals. Procedural functions served to support those goals.

Each city studied has distinct housing/community development goals that are manifested in the implementation of urban homesteading. The Urban Homesteading Program came to represent one tool available to city officials. The goal of urban homesteading had to fit into the larger context of the housing/ community development goals.

The Detroit and Philadelphia Section 810 programs aimed to provide low- and moderate-income home opportunities and to stabilize communities. Detroit directed its local program toward a higher-income population. Urban homesteading is not a key element in the current community development/housing strategy; hence, its implementation is not a priority. The urban homesteading focus on low- and moderate-income persons in Philadelphia apparently originated after 1978, when the city assumed the program. Indications are that it will remain a part of housing- and community-development policy in the near future. A clearly stated objective of Baltimore's community development/housing policy is to attract middle-income persons back into the city, and urban homesteading was a step toward attaining this goal.

Economic and commercial development is a priority in Detroit's community development strategy; however, urban homesteading did not assume a prominent position in achieving those goals. The program is not a major effort within the implementing agency, nor is it particularly identified with Mayor Young. Targeting the program to low- and moderate-income households does not suggest any immediate economic benefit; however, reoccupying vacant homes may eventually provide spin-off benefits to the neighborhoods and long-term economic opportunity to the homesteaders. To many observers, economic development in Detroit has become synonymous with downtown redevelopment. The objective of increasing the upper-income population is addressed there through such efforts as the construction of market-rate apartment buildings in the Central Business

District.   The reluctance of the city administration to
implement the Nuisance Abatement   Ordinance because of
possible unconstitutionality suggests   caution in proceeding
with innovative ideas that have doubtful economic benefit.
     A strong tradition of economic development has not been
displayed in Philadelphia, although it must certainly be a
fiscal concern.   In the other two cities,   long-serving
mayors have influenced the direction of development.   This
corroborates Dommel's finding based on case studies   in New
Haven,   Chicago,   and Boston--mayors were often prime movers
and dominant figures in urban renewal programs.[12] Due to
provisions in the Philadelphia city charter that limit re-
election to two terms,   three mayors have held office during
the time that Baltimore and Detroit had just one mayor.   A
shorter term limits opportunities for mayoral   influence.
While the urban homesteading program has--by virtue of its
production--made inroads in providing housing to the target
population, it has not done so within the context of a broad
policy.   Mayor Goode's efforts in Philadelphia to reorganize
and increase the accountability of the OHCD were attempts to
correct the troubled community development environment.
     Providing low- and moderate-income housing is a priority
evident   in the   PHDC's mandate.   When targeted   so
specifically,   the needs of this population are less likely
to be ignored.   The city has been willing to implement the
controversial Nuisance Abatement Program to further serve
low- and moderate-income objectives in spite of possible
legal challenges.
     In Baltimore,   where economic development   is the
prevailing goal,   urban homesteading aimed to achieve
increases in the tax base.   Bolstering the tax base by
attracting upwardly mobile,   young professionals was part of
the official strategy.   A stated objective of the city
administration was to build a "Baltimore that would provide
better housing for its low and middle income families, with
innovative residential programs that would lure suburbanites
back into the city."[13]
     Baltimore's   selection of a higher-income   target
population created a number of possibilities.   Houses
requiring substantial rehabilitation   were utilized and
homesteaders could afford to contract for repairs or perform
them with sweat equity.   The city garnered financial support
through a city bond sale to provide rehabilitation loans.
Shorter periods of residence were required,   increasing the
local homesteading program's economic appeal.   On the other
hand,   the criteria accompanying the federal program did not
fit well with local purposes.   The lure of a few eligible
properties   did   not   reduce   the   city's disfavor   of
regulations.
     To what extent urban homesteading may have caused
displacement or gentrification in Baltimore neighborhoods is
uncertain.   However,   the overall benefit of housing- and
community-development programs must be gauged against the
costs to persons who are displaced.   The National Urban
Coalition warned that a strengthened tax base and some gains
in residential and commercial revitalization could clash

with the creation of new urban nomads.[14] A study funded by
HUD documented that private reinvestment has produced some
benefits for   cities but also has   adversely affected
households in the neighborhoods prior to the beginning of
reinvestment.[15]

DHCD official Thomas Jaudon claims that Baltimore has
not ignored its low- and moderate-income population.   He
stated that the   city had found new   construction of
low/moderate units using UDAG funds more cost-effective than
rehabilitation.   Recent UDAG data seem to support this
assertion.   During fiscal year 1983, Baltimore received
$3.76 million of   UDAG funds for   construction   or
rehabilitation of housing for low- and moderate-income
persons in eight projects. Six economic and commercial
development projects were awarded $2.54 million: that is, 60
percent of   the funds   were directed   to lower-income
households.   By contrast, housing projects nationwide
receive 11 percent of UDAG funds. None of Detroit's 1983
UDAG allocation of $10,671,155 was directed toward low- and
moderate-income housing.   Philadelphia received $12 million
in UDAG grants in 1983; one $2 million renovation project
required the provision of 20 percent of the total units for
low- and moderate-income persons (about 4 percent of the
UDAG total).

No comprehensive study of Urban Homesteading Programs
has been conducted since the demonstration program
evaluation completed in 1980.   The impact of urban
homesteading upon all segments of each community is a
variable that must be assessed in determining overall
success.   Unique, specific organizational goals inhibit a
parallel comparison among cities.   It may be more feasible
to examine the respective alignment of organizational goals
and their environments.   Detroit's goal of assisting low-
and moderate-income persons could not be achieved with the
resources and support provided.   Baltimore's political and
economic environment was conducive to its middle-income
focus.   Philadelphia's officials successfully manipulated
the available resources toward meeting the city's low- and
moderate-income targeting goal.

FEDERAL INPUT INTO LOCAL PROGRAMS

Federal Funding

Fluctuations in urban homesteading authorizations since
1975 reflect the tenuous status of the program nationally
over the years.   There have been lags in appropriations,
allocations, and expenditures since its inception.   Between
1975 and 1980, Congress appropriated $55 million to support
the acquisition of Section 810 properties.   Between 1980 to
1982, no appropriations occurred.   Unexpended appropriations
were sufficient to operate the program at a level comparable
to previous years.   HUD staffers attribute the slowdown to
the time required for programs under the new operating
status to become functional.

For fiscal year 1988, Congress appropriated $14.4 million to urban homesteading, increasing the overall total to $129.4 million since 1975. The amount of an allocation is based on the expected number of available HUD and VA properties in the community that would be suitable for homesteading, the average as-is value of HUD properties in jurisdiction, and the timeliness and cost-effectiveness of the community's past performance.[16] By the end of fiscal 1985, $84.171 million of Section 810 funds--or 92 percent of cumulative appropriations to that point--had been expended. Of that amount, $12.205 million was spent during fiscal 1985. Section 810 allocations to the subject cities for the past six years are shown in Table 7.1.

Section 312 loans constituted the principal source of rehabilitation funding in the program. Congress has made no new appropriations for the Section 312 Program since 1981. The program has been financed entirely from loan repayments, recovery of prior years' commitments, and the unobligated balance left from previous years. HUD assigned Section 312 funding for single-family rehabilitation solely to HUD-approved urban homesteading areas in 1982 and 1983. Eligible properties included both Section 810 and non-homesteading dwellings located in approved homesteading areas. In fiscal 1983, loans amounting to $44.86 million were awarded through the program. Of that sum, 598 loans totaling $11.46 million were distributed for single-family residences in homesteading areas. Three-fifths of the single-family amount went to homesteaders; the balance went to other homeowners in homesteading areas. The renewed emphasis on urban homesteading in funding priority was accompanied by new legislative initiatives as well in the Housing and Urban-Rural Recovery Act of 1983.

Restrictions have not been imposed on the types of properties eligible to receive Section 312 funds since fiscal 1983. A comparison of 1983 and 1985 reveals a distinct difference in the types of properties rehabilitated with Section 312 funds. In fiscal 1983, 26 percent of Section 312 assistance went to single-family properties and 74 percent to multi-family properties. By contrast, in fiscal 1985, 78 percent went to single-family properties and 22 percent went to owners of other properties. Of $75.007 million obligated for loans during 1985, $10.4 million, or slightly less than 14, percent was used in the rehabilitation of urban homesteading 470 units. For 294 of these units, Section 312 was the sole source of financing, totaling $6.2 million; for 176 units, Section 312 funds of $4.1 million was combined with other sources. Hence, while Section 312 remained a major source for urban homesteading financing, Section 810 urban homesteading was no longer a major focus of Section 312 funding.

Federal-Local Interaction

Two sources of information provide the material for this discussion of interaction between federal and state

		TABLE 7.1 SECTION 810 ALLOCATIONS			
CITY	1982	1983	1984	1985	1986-88
Baltimore	$ 75,000	$ 75,000	$ 0	$ 0	$ 0
Detroit	340,000	325,000	83,570	0	0
Philadelphia	300,000	300,000	416,000	118,900	270,000

officials: HUD area office monitoring letters of the Section 810 Program and interviews with participating officials. Monitoring of the Section 810 Urban Homesteading Program for accountability is left to the discretion of the area office. Monitoring runs the spectrum from intensive (in Philadelphia) to minimal (in Detroit).   Some differences observed among the cities were certainly due to individual personalities, but others reflect established patterns of relationships between the levels of government.   Those city representatives with extensive experience in dealing with federal programs are more likely to view federal officials favorably than those without such experience.[17]

Federal and local officials form images of one another that influence the perceptions of individuals within their organizations.   These images affect the interaction between officials and the negotiating positions that officials on each side take.[18] Characterizations of federal, state, and local officials indicate that national officials judge local officials as holding a highly restricted, particularistic, even parochial, set of perspectives.[19] Different perspectives among officials at various levels in the intergovernmental process are not unexpected.   Differences have also been noted in perception between one official and another at the same level.[20] Perceptions and images are important in the monitoring of Section 810 because it was very much influenced by the individual monitor.

Philadelphia. The extensive monitoring in Philadelphia may
stem from the previous unsatisfactory experience with the
nonprofit Urban Homesteading Board   as   an implementing
agency.   Correspondence between the HUD area office and the
city of Philadelphia, in which the city was strongly advised
to monitor the program through its Monitoring and Program
Evaluation Division in the OHCD supports this contention.
This places the city in a position of greater responsibility
for the program.
      Philadelphia's monitoring since 1982 has raised concerns
about management controls,   nonconformity with regulatory
requirements,   and deficiencies in rehabilitation work.
Techniques have included site visits as well as inspections
of rehabilitated properties.   A series of detailed letters
between the city and HUD attempted to resolve numerous
matters, including the three-month suspension of the program
in 1982.   One letter, dated July 3,   1983, highlighted
problems of fragmented administration (there had been rapid
turnover in staff, causing a lack of continuity and program
knowledge);   inaccurate records (leading to inadequate
control over the program); and poor productivity.   Only
forty-six cases had been completed in an eighteen-month
period: an average of two and one-half per month, less than
two per staff person per year.   The performance criterion
used by the Philadelphia HUD area office is twenty-five
cases per staff person per year.[21] The city of Philadelphia
was ordered to reimburse the Section 810 fund $22,000 for
another violation.   HUD guidelines require that localities
obtain prior approval to use properties purchased with
Section 810 money in some other way.   Two such properties
were conveyed to squatters and one was used in the city's
1202A Program.   The latter program allows an individual
licensed by the city to enter and make repairs on a vacant,
privately-owned, tax delinquent property.   PHDC's procedures
were in direct violation of program conditions; hence, the
sanction was applied.
      In addition to the program, the implementing agency has
been criticized.   The Philadelphia HUD area office
coordinator seemed rather intolerant of PHDC and its
operation.   He criticized the "laundry list" of programs
available and felt that they may "cause more confusion than
anything else."   He granted that the agency was good at
producing units when it was operating and applauded the
current urban homesteading administrator.   He attributed
continuing problems to the bureaucratic hierarchy and
communication problems between PHDC and the city
administration.[22]
      The PHDC staff voiced concerns about HUD's slow response
time, citing periods of up to one year for the official
transfer of properties.   The resourceful PHDC homesteading
director indicated that he had managed to maneuver around
that obstacle too--in a fashion he did not disclose.   The
homesteading director also noted two other problems.   The
first, excessive paperwork and lengthy processing times, is
endemic to federal/local relations.   The second, the period
between conditional conveyance and final conveyance of title

(now five years) has hampered the willingness of
conservative lenders to provide rehabilitation loans. The
issue of contention concerns the lender's ability to
foreclose during this period. The city apparently will not
participate in the new HUD urban homesteading demonstrations
because "they don't offer anything."[23] On the contrary,
Section 810 does offer something to the city. And PHDC, the
city administration, and HUD have made steady, but often
conflicting, progress to achieve it. Plans to include two
additional neighborhoods indicate the acceptance of this
program. Urban homesteading is seen as an important
component of the city's response to prioritize homeownership
providing homeownership opportunities to low- and moderate-
income families.

Baltimore. The Baltimore Section 810 Program has reached an
amicable conclusion. During the entire period of its
operation, however, monitoring occurred. The monitoring was
slightly less thorough than in Philadelphia, and no
rehabilitation inspections were made. Compared to
Philadelphia, the tone of correspondence was less adverse;
no punitive action was threatened or taken. The Baltimore
HUD office suggested an administrative change to establish a
line organization within the Homeownership Division of the
DHCD; it was accepted. The rather detailed correspondence
between HUD and DHCD primarily concerned the timely
completion of properties. The Baltimore Section 810 Program
encountered what appear to be routine problems with some
homesteaders' inability to secure financing, contractor
delays or nonselection, credit matters, and withdrawals.
The significant point is that the HUD area office maintained
constant watch over each property.
     Though initiated by HUD, the decision to close out the
Section 810 Program was mutually agreeable. It was due to
(1) the economics of urban homesteading, which changed
during the six years of operation in Park Heights; (2) lack
of eligible properties; and (3) marketing problems caused by
the high costs of rehabilitation in a community that did not
attract people with sufficient incomes. From the standpoint
of the HUD area office, the problems were beyond anyone's
control.[24] HUD has commended the city for its pioneering
spirit in many community development programs, although the
Park Heights urban homesteading project did not fare well.
HUD's urban homesteading manager noted a tendency within the
DHCD to bend rules; this did not occur with urban
homesteading, however, because the small scale of the
program allowed for close scrutiny.
     The administrator of the DHCD Homeownership Division--
which ran urban homesteading--downplayed the significance of
the Section 810 Program as compared to the local program,
commenting that it "was almost a headache to do."[25] At the
heart of this allegation was the view that HUD charged too
much for the properties and did not offer anything except
some Section 312 loan funds for renovation. The cost
complaint was peculiar to Baltimore and may reflect its
objective of attracting upper-income households to more

expensive properties.   The program was costly to the city,
which subsidized the property cost.   Perhaps in this same
spirit of insufficient incentives, Baltimore has declined to
participate in both the new single-family, city-owned urban
homesteading   demonstration   and   the   multi-family
demonstration.

Detroit.   The level of federal oversight exercised in the
Baltimore and Philadelphia cases differs greatly from that
in Detroit.   The first and only monitoring report was made
in April 1985--although Detroit has been a participant in
the Section 810 Urban Homesteading Program since 1979.   That
report belatedly questioned the fundamental elements of the
program: the   target   areas   selected   and   the   income
eligibility standards for homesteader selection.   The report
observed that while most homesteading activity had occurred
in the northside area,   the area is so large that the impact
of housing repairs and other neighborhood improvement could
be insignificant.   diluted.   The scarcity of homesteading
activity in the westside area led HUD officials to question
its suitability for the program.   HUD officials subtly
suggested that the city modify the target neighborhoods to
enhance program   impact.   This   action would   require
submission of a revised application to the area office for
review and approval.
    Local program guidelines for Section 810 set an income-
eligibility limit   of $25,000   for urban homesteading
families.   HUD officials found the standard rigid, since it
does not consider adjustments for family size.   As a
consequence,   potentially eligible   households that are
moderate income,   by definition,   could be excluded from the
program.   In this case, HUD again mildly suggested revisions
to the local guidelines.
    HUD questioned the following areas of performance:

    1. Timeliness of processing cases from start
        (property acquisition/homesteader selection)
        to finish (the conveyance of fee simple title
        to the homesteader).   The multiple inspection
        process employing both   the Department of
        Buildings and   Safety and   the CEDD   was
        criticized.   HUD   acknowledges that   this
        process is required by local ordinance in the
        monitoring report.   No attempt was made to
        intervene in local policymaking to revise it;
        however,   a   suggestion   was   made   for
        modification within the existing structure.
        In addition,   the city was not in compliance
        with program rules to transfer fee simple
        title to homesteaders after three years (prior
        to the change to five years).   Only on this
        matter did HUD insist upon correction.
    2. Management Information Systems diverted staff
        time   from program   management to report
        maintenance.   CEDD staff   was   allegedly

preparing   numerous   automated   and   manual
reports for   different purposes   and each   was
found   to   have different   data   requirements,
time frames, and formats.
3.   Quality of repairs.   Deficiencies were found
in each of three properties fully inspected.

HUD officials   complimented city   staff responsible   for
urban homesteading   implementation.   The   monitoring report
was less   critical and threatening   than those   prepared for
either Baltimore or Philadelphia.   The tenor of communication   between Detroit   and the   area   office may   eventually
change for two reasons.   First,   a more permanent HUD staff
may   result in   more   consistent   monitoring and   follow-up.
Three   persons have   held   this   position since   1979;   the
current individual has been in   place only since March 1985.
Second,   future   monitoring   correspondence   may   reflect
inevitable   tension   between   HUD and   city   officials   over
specific recommendations.   HUD may   more adamantly   pursue
changes by   the city with regard   to those matters   it deems
important.   Monitoring correspondence between   HUD and city
officials in   the other   two cities   became more   pointed as
deliberations   ensued.   Notably,   the   Detroit   monitoring
report concludes with a comment   that supports the notion of
program linkage:

Since   there is   a tie-in   between the   city's
Urban   Homesteading   program,   its   CDBG
rehabilitation   program,   and   its   Section   312
rehabilitation   loan program   we   believe an   even
greater return   will be   received for   any efforts
invested   in   improving   Section   810   program
management.[26]

Until the 1985 monitoring report, Detroit urban homesteading
staff had little contact with   the HUD area office officials
beyond submitting quarterly progress   reports.   The absence
of   regular   monitoring   seemed mutually   agreeable.   The
relationship   has since   been terse.   The   city's lack of
productivity   has   been   called   into   question   because
properties   were never   conveyed,   even conditionally,   to
homesteaders.   The city has not requested additional Section
810 funds   since fiscal   year 1984.   The Detroit   HUD area
office remains a reluctant overseer on this program.
Like Baltimore and Philadelphia,   Detroit does not plan
to   participate in   the   two   new   urban   homesteading
demonstrations.   Perhaps   with Section   810   in   mind,
restrictive regulations and duplication of existing programs
were cited as the reasons.
In   summary,   Section   810   urban homesteading   afforded
significant discretion to the HUD area offices as well as to
the implementing   agencies.   Discretion,   however,   is not
synonymous with   autonomy.   The   significant   oversight
exercised in   Baltimore and   Philadelphia demonstrates   that
cities may   have been allowed   to make their   own decisions,
but they   were still subject   to scrutiny.   This situation
countermands the   supposed advantages   of discretion.   The

fact that all three cities declined to participate in two
new federal urban homesteading initiatives may indicate a
measure of dissatisfaction with the limited discretion
actually available.   Freedom from red tape, paperwork, and
regulations seem to be foremost considerations in the minds
of local officials relative to federal programs.

INSIGNIFICANT   VARIABLES: HOUSING   STOCK   AND   CITIZEN
PARTICIPATION

Although housing characteristics and community input have
been discussed,   neither is a major determinant of urban
homesteading implementation at the   local level.   All
Baltimore and Philadelphia urban homesteading properties
were attached row houses of masonry construction;   Detroit's
have been detached single-family homes, primarily of brick
construction, with some frame buildings.   One national HUD
official commented that the row house construction type may
be more suitable for rehabilitation than demolition since an
individual rowhouse cannot be demolished--the fates of the
units are linked.   However, the choice of housing--like the
choice of target area--is an outgrowth of program goals.
Though one might assume that rowhouses are more appropriate
for   urban   homesteading   than   single-family   detached
properties because relative costs are less, reported urban
homesteading rehabilitation   costs $15,000   in Detroit;
$25,000   to $30,000   in   Baltimore;   and $20,000   in
Philadelphia--which may reduce the advantage.
     Citizen participation is not a major component of the
Urban Homesteading Program.   HUD requires only that the
community be informed of the program;   the actual mechanics
are left up to the locality.   Urban homesteading boards in
the subject cities have become functionally irrelevant.   The
independent board in Philadelphia was terminated when the
city assumed the program in 1978.   The need for boards in
Baltimore dissipated with the slowdown and impending close-
out of the program.   The advisory board in one Detroit urban
homesteading community continues to operate marginally with
five members--the other is inactive.   The lack of strong
citizen participation requirements is related to the
discretionary nature of the program as well as to its
relative size and scale.

CONCLUSION

The Urban Homesteading Programs   enacted by each city
differed in important ways from the federal programs.   In
Baltimore, the federal project was not major, contrasting
with the pivotal local effort.   In Detroit, the local
program focussed on the higher-income bracket while the
federal one was targeted to low-income households.   The
local and federal initiatives in Philadelphia were run
primarily by nonprofit organizations characterized by staff
turnover.   These and other differences discussed in this

chapter greatly influenced the operation of the Urban Homesteading Programs.

Section 810 enabled cities to develop program goals that addressed local conditions. Specific goals and various other factors have influenced program results. This study has not labeled "good" or "bad" implementation, but contains observations--some peculiar to this program, others more generalized--to contribute to the ongoing body of work on implementation. The urban homesteading concept may be simple, but its execution is not. The final chapter explores some theoretical implications and policy recommendations based on these case studies.

NOTES

1. Paul Berman, "The Study of Macro- and Micro-Implementation," Public Policy 26 (Spring 1978), 178.

2. Ibid.

3. Interview with Paul Dornan, HUD, National Headquarters, October 15, 1984.

4. Anthony Downs, Inside Bureaucracy (Boston: Little, Brown, 1967), p. 134.

5. Ibid., p. 153

6. "Fourth Annual Report on the Urban Homesteading Program" (unpublished), p. 52.

7. Jeffrey L. Pressman, Federal Programs and City Politics (Berkeley and Los Angeles: University of California Press, 1975), p. 12.

8. Roberto Brambilla and Gianni Longo, Learning from Baltimore (New York: Institute for Environmental Action, 1979), p. 71.

9. Interview with Thomas Jaudon, Baltimore Department of Housing and Community Development, November 28, 1984.

10. Interview with Julia Robinson, Philadelphia Office of Housing, November 15, 1984.

11. The New York Times, January 1, 1980, p. 12.

12. Paul R. Dommel, et al., Decentralizing Urban Policy (Washington, D.C.: The Brookings Institution, 1982), p. 22.

13. City of Baltimore, Annual Report, 1976, p. 11.

14. The National Urban Coalition, Displacement: City Neighborhoods in Transition (Washington, D.C., The National Urban Coalition, 1978), p. 1.

15. Frank F. DeGiovanni, "An Examination of Selection Consequences of Revitalization in Six U.S. Cities," Urban Studies 21 (August 1984), 245-59.

16. HUD, Office of Community Planning and Development, Consolidated Annual Report to Congress on Community Development Programs, p. 110.

17. Pressman, Federal Programs, p. 97.

18. Ibid. p. 86.

19. Deil S. Wright, Understanding Intergovernmental Relations (Belmont, California: Wadsworth Publishing Company, 1978), pp. 64-65.

20. Pressman, Federal Programs, p. 97.

21. Community Development Block Grant monitoring letter, June 4, 1984.

22. Interview with Stephen Rhodeside, HUD, Philadelphia Area Office, November 15, 1984.

23. Interview with Vincent Coles, Philadelphia Housing Development Corporation, November 15, 1984.

24. Interview with Ellsworth Andrews, HUD, Baltimore Area Office, November 28, 1984.

25. Interview with Thomas Jaudon.

26. HUD monitoring letter, April 19, 1985.

8

Theoretical Implications and Policy Recommendations

The implementation of Urban Homesteading Programs in Baltimore, Detroit, and Philadelphia provided an opportunity to examine the most widely publicized, narrow-purpose categorical program for housing. That program, Section 810 Urban Homesteading, is distinguished by its enactment in an era of decentralization and block grants. This chapter examines (1) the achievement of desired outcomes through the implementation process (macro-implementation) and (2) the factors that affected the implementation itself (micro-implementation).

The macro-implementation problem was twofold: failure to provide operational and administrative support and restrictive mandates. The former resulted in funding choices among various programs that were detrimental to Section 810. In an environment of scarce resources such choices must be made. In the latter case, locally enacted urban homesteading and other programs did not have the baggage of the federal program and could be pursued in a fashion more consistent with local goals.

Although numerous factors influenced micro-implementation, three were most significant in the case of Section 810: organizational capacity, political/financial support, and local goals. The comprehensive umbrella organization in Baltimore had the most consistent approach to its programs; Detroit's structure was least supportive; and Philadelphia's quasi-public agency posed some unique problems. Baltimore and Philadelphia had different goals, yet political and financial support was apparent in both cities. The Detroit program did not enjoy either. Attainment of local goals was compounded by the other two factors. Targeting middle- and upper-income groups (Baltimore) placed fewer demands upon public support. Targeting lower-income groups (Detroit and Philadelphia) generated additional pressure for public support. Philadelphia was better prepared institutionally to address the needs of this population. Each of these factors are discussed below with others that relate specifically or generally to the implementation of urban homesteading.

INTERGOVERNMENTAL POLICY IMPLICATIONS

Intergovernmental policy has provided the backdrop for the struggle between ensuring national intent and allowing local autonomy. Efforts to implement Section 810 Urban Homesteading demonstrate the complexity of intergovernmental policy. Urban homesteading could be an ideal policy--one that specifies an intended national purpose but allows some local initiative. This local input would presumably enhance program impact. Section 810 attempted to meld the two interests without yielding maximum results. So the drawbacks of both centralization and decentralization were manifested in this program's operation in the processes of macro- and micro-implementation.

The major centralization concern is incompatibility of national directives with local situations. Two aspects of Section 810 legislation that conflicted most with local preferences were neighborhood targeting and program coordination. These two mandates limited the range of implementation possibilities.

A concern of decentralization--that localities would deviate from intended (explicit or implicit) objectives was also observed. In Philadelphia, directives were purposefully disregarded when contrary to local preferences. In Baltimore, the program was not utilized due to inconsonance with local realities. These specific circumstances are discussed below.

Section 810 deviated from the standard categorical program by allowing local governments the flexibility to design their own programs (implementation processes) and set their own goals (measures of attainment). This discretion gave rise to the questions that initiated this research. This chapter discusses the variables of program success; the significance of discretion; the factors accounting for variation in implementation outcomes; and possible recommendations for urban homesteading specifically and federal programs generally.

FEDERAL AND LOCAL GOALS: A MEASURE OF SUCCESS

It is difficult to uniformly evaluate the success of urban homesteading implementation in Baltimore, Detroit, and Philadelphia. During the early days of homesteading, some pragmatists cautioned that it was no panacea for blighted buildings and run down neighborhoods. The program's overall redeeming quality was the possibility that personal commitment and hard labor, in carefully selected areas, could succeed where bureaucracies had and could not. A 1973 Washington Post editorial commented that "homesteading will be worthwhile if it injects even small portions of new life, energy and imagination into the urban scene."[1]

There is no uniform standard to measure the success of Section 810 Urban Homesteading because the program did not include an explicit statement of goals. Policies normally contain both goals and the means of achieving them.[2]

Implementation can be defined as the ability to forge
subsequent links in the causal chain so as to obtain the
desired results.[3] Participating localities supplied their
own goals to complete the Section 810 policy statement; the
legislation provided the means: vacant houses. The three
cities developed different approaches for linking actions to
objectives. Hence, the goals must be individually and
collectively assessed.

Although the cities' goals were unique, their programs
strived for one or more of the following: (1) to reduce HUD
and other federally owned vacant property (production); (2)
to provide homeownership opportunities to low- and moderate-
income persons; and (3) to expand the tax base by attracting
upper-income persons into the city.

The first goal, held primarily by HUD, was only achieved
in part. Section 810 made a very small dent in the
inventory of vacant properties nationwide. HUD's national
holdings decreased significantly from a high point of 75,000
at the end of fiscal year 1974 to 16,432 by the end of
fiscal year 1985. Transfers to local urban homesteading
programs accounted for less than 3 percent of all HUD
properties disposed of between 1975 and 1983.[4] Further, HUD-
owned Section 810 properties accounted for about 1 percent
of all HUD-acquired properties sold during fiscal year
1985.[5] Changes in HUD inventory for the subject cities shown
in Table 8.1 confirm the marginal impact of Section 810.

Detroit and Philadelphia both espoused the goal of
social targeting in carrying out Section 810. The results
in Detroit have been inconsequential--hardly a success from
anyone's standpoint. Neither federal nor local goals have
been met. Few low- and moderate-income benefits have been
realized; prospective beneficiaries have been dissatisfied
with the program. Public and private resources were
apparently unavailable to Detroit officials to achieve
lower-income homeownership goals. Yet the implementation
plan was not changed. The political benefits of targeting
the program to this constituency have been unrealized.

Philadelphia has demonstrated the capacity to surpass
Detroit in its urban homesteading efforts, having produced
five times more homesteads. Recent Section 810 allocations
to both cities are instructive. The 1984 allocation for
Detroit dropped from $325,000 in 1983 to $83,570;
Philadelphia's increased from $300,000 to $416,000 for the
same period. HUD gauges performance by measuring progress,
that is, the rate at which recipients spend their money.
Those who spend more receive more through allocations.

Philadelphia's urban homesteading production record has
better served the target population than that of Detroit.
Programs to provide housing for low-and moderate-income
persons have been institutionalized. That is the raison
d'etre for the PHDC and a major reason for the higher
production rate.

Urban homesteading in Baltimore became a tool for
bolstering the tax base, a part of the city's comprehensive
development strategy. A higher income homesteading population spared the city the financial problems encountered

TABLE 8.1
CROSSCUTTING REGULATIONS

	Social/Economic		Administrative/Fiscal		Total	
	N	%	N	%	N	%
Prior to 1960	4	11	2	9	6	10
1960s	9	25	9	39	18	31
1970s	23	64	12	52	35	59
Total	36	100	23	100	59	100

SOURCE: The Regulation of American Federalism, pp. 43-44, Kettle, as derived from U.S. Office of Management and Budget, Managing Federal Assistance in the 1980s, Working Papers, Vol. 1, (Washington, D.C.).

in Detroit.   Baltimore succeeded to some extent in meeting its urban homesteading objective through the   local program not the federal Section 810 program.   The overall community development effort--including the use of UDAGs and other programs to meet the housing needs of lower-income segments of the population--must be assessed as well.   Housing efforts   should   be   attentive   to   all   sectors   of   the population.
     Section 810's potential impact in each city has always been limited by the federal government's scarce allocation of funds.   Baltimore and Philadelphia achieved some measure of success while Detroit did not.   The success of urban homesteading in all three cities, however, can be called into question.   Although HUD managed to greatly reduce its vacant holdings,   urban homesteading accounted for a small percentage of the decrease (except in Baltimore, where the total volume was low).   Abandoned properties continue to blight urban neighborhoods, and low- and moderate-income persons are still underhoused.   Insufficient local tax revenue remains an important urban fiscal concern.

DISCRETION GIVEN AND TAKEN AWAY

To provide program flexibility, HUD's express intention
was to develop administration guidelines rather than program
regulations for Section 810.   However, based upon Kettl's
categorization   of   rules   affecting   programs,   it   is
questionable that this intent was achieved.   Kettl has
categorized federal rules as follows:

1. Those that must be followed as a condition of
   funding;
2. Those   that decide   who program   beneficiaries
   should be; and
3. Those that eliminate "fraud, waste, and abuse"
   from federal programs.[6]

Ultimately,   each   type of rule became   a component of
urban homesteading.   Only   on   the   decision   of program
beneficiaries did Congress refrain from rule making until
the 1983 legislation requiring priority for lower-income
persons.   Even under the guise of discretion, "the federal
government   never   gives   away   money   without   strings
attached."[7]
Federal urban homesteading regulations purported to
allow considerable flexibility to communities in setting up
their programs.   HUD afforded major discretion to the cities
in setting overall program goals.   Secondarily, communities
could adopt different approaches to homesteader selection,
property choice,   and rehabilitation financing mechanisms.
However, the prescription of key components (targeting and
coordination),   by establishing the operational context,
impedes discretion.   As a consequence, program mechanics
differed only slightly to meet local goals.   Both discretion
and constraint were significant in Baltimore, Detroit, and
Philadelphia.
Officials in all three cities found Section 810 program
criteria objectionable.   The apparent reason for this stems
from the characteristics of federal-local interaction and--
more importantly--the essence of categorical programs.   It
is difficult to reconcile the concurrent pursuit of federal
objectives and the maintenance of local control; political
debate and administrative controversy have surrounded the
issue.   Section 810 Urban Homesteading is a product of that
dilemma.   Adopted in the same legislative package as CDBG,
it combined elements of discretion within a categorical
framework.   The elements of categoricalism have given rise
to some local objections.   Discretion in Section 810 Urban
Homesteading is tempered by the narrow focus of the program,
the competitive application and pre-approval process, annual
renewal, cross cutting regulations, and program monitoring.

Narrow Purpose

Urban homesteading's federal purpose was, and is, to utilize existing housing stock to provide homeownership, thereby encouraging public and private investment in selected neighborhoods and assisting in their preservation and revitalization.[8] The legislation's definition of eligible properties is a limitation because only federally owned properties in HUD-approved local urban homesteading areas can be transferred to participating localities.

Incremental legislative changes highlight the significance of those restraints. Earlier changes expanded the scope of eligible properties to include vacant properties held by the VA and the FHA as well as those held by HUD. A new single-family Urban Homesteading Demonstration Program, legislated as Section 810(i), allows the use of federal funds to purchase other local properties. The Housing and Urban-Rural Act of 1983 authorized a Local Property Urban Homesteading Demonstration Program to test the feasibility of acquiring properties locally for use in homesteading. These amendments and legislative initiatives have broadened the scope of urban homesteading. Its impact on neighborhood revitalization may be enhanced by the inclusion of more property types. In addition, the local versions of the program created a spectrum of possibilities. For example, Detroit's as-is effort was a response to demands for broader application to other neighborhoods. Nuisance Abatement legislation to authorize squatting in Detroit and Philadelphia is another offshoot of the urban homesteading concept.

Application and Pre-approval Process

Urban homesteading differs markedly from CDBG in regard to application and pre-approval processes. Section 810 funds are not awarded until a competitive application detailing plans for coordinated development and improvement, rehabilitation financing, and implementation is submitted and approved. Cities are only required to submit an application at the program's outset; amendments are filed during subsequent years to reflect changes. By comparison, CDBG is an entitlement program: applications from eligible jurisdictions are automatically approved, unless HUD raises objections within seventy-five days after submission. These terms are set forth in the Housing and Community Development Act of 1974. In keeping with the decentralization focus of CDBG, HUD area offices--rather than the Washington office-- approve both CDBG and urban homesteading applications. The HUD area offices did not raise any objections during the urban homesteading application review process of the three cities studied.

Crosscutting Regulations

Urban homesteading has been subject to a number of regulations that apply across the board to many, if not all, federal grant programs. The number of rules has grown steadily since 1960 and includes procedural rules for grant coordination, administrative and fiscal rules, and social and economic rules. Table 8.1 presents a brief tabulation of crosscutting regulations. The proliferation of federal restraints that get attached to grants has been coined "flypaper federalism."[9] Among the complaints from state and local sources are that (1) pervasive federal regulation is choking effective governance at the local level and (2) the fiscal dependency and federal restrictions have severely curtailed the program priorities of local government. The disparity of goals between programmatic federal officials and politically sensitive local leaders explains disagreement over many categoricals.[10]

Among the rules and regulations applicable to urban homesteading have been A-95 clearinghouse review,[11] non-discrimination, national environmental policy, lead-based paint procedures, and acquisition and relocation policy. These regulations and others also applied to the more encompassing CDBG program. The compliance of Urban Homesteading implementers was likely, as they depended upon CDBG for operating funds. Nonetheless, the inclusion of crosscutting regulations in Section 810 legislation erodes regulatory discretion.

Program Monitoring for Control

Program monitoring of Section 810 occurred at the discretion of the HUD area offices; its use as a control device varied in the subject cities. Clearly, monitoring played an important role in the Baltimore and Philadelphia programs and in the relationships among federal and local officials. Maximization of the monitoring role may be more typical than minimization--as in the case of Detroit. Monitoring officials tend to become advocates of greater control over the operating bureaus because they wish to perform their function better and because it increases their significance. Such officials may agitate for more detailed reports from operating bureaus and demand ever-greater limitations on bureau discretion.[12] The production of reports and records to facilitate monitoring can generate additional costs to the operating agency and create another impediment to program participation and cooperation. Performance monitoring has been criticized for its cen-tralization aspects in an era of decentralization. When used, it can effectively supplant the element of local flexibility provided in the program guidelines.[13]

In sum, urban homesteading implementors had flexibility in a major area, that is, goal setting. Full use of that discretion was not possible due to conditions attached to categorical and other federal programs.

APPLICATIONS TO THEORY AND POLICY

The experiences of Baltimore, Detroit, and Philadelphia in urban homesteading implementation confirm some propositions about intergovernmental relations, federal influence on localities, political influence, goal divergencies, mutual adaptation advanced in other studies of public policy and administration. Moreover, program outcomes are often more related to the specific characteristics of the cities and programs involved than to general theories related to federal programs and their implementation. These findings naturally form the basis for future study and policy making. Some research directions and policy recommendations follow.

Urban Homesteading: Commonalities with Other Federal Programs

This study of urban homesteading as a federal program supports the following conclusions about federal program implementation found in the existing literature:

1. <u>Interdependence</u> and <u>variable control</u> <u>are</u> <u>elements</u> <u>of</u> <u>federal</u> <u>programs</u>. The pendulum swings back and forth between centralization and decentralization as the focus on local autonomy and national objectives changes. Even though urban homesteading was to provide discretion within a categorical framework, elements of federal control manifested themselves. Performance monitoring, annual reviews, and cross cutting regulations are the main techniques currently in use.

Cities rely upon the federal government for resources--in this case, houses--to carry out programs. Conversely, the federal government depends upon local governments to run Urban Homesteading Programs. The degree of federal dependence varies from one domestic function to another. Community development depends heavily upon local initiative.[14] Yet when the federal purpose, such as social targeting, is not achieved, mandatory requirements have been imposed on localities. Section 810 is a case in point.

2. A <u>policy</u> <u>entrepreneur</u> <u>or</u> <u>other</u> <u>interested</u> <u>government</u> <u>official</u> <u>can</u> <u>significantly</u> <u>influence</u> <u>the</u> <u>course</u> <u>of</u> <u>a</u> <u>public</u> <u>policy</u>. Programs that depend upon local initiative are extremely vulnerable to the vicissitudes of local politics.[15] The locally enacted program in Baltimore had the administrative support of then Department of Housing and Community Development Director Robert Embry and the political support of Mayor William Schaefer. With a clear goal in mind

for the application of urban homesteading, the
city could forge ahead with its program to target
middle-income households while almost totally
avoiding criticism from the lower-income
population. The federal program, conversely, did
not meld with local objectives; hence, political
priority was not forthcoming. Philadelphia's
locally enacted program--due to the support of the
city council, led by Joseph Coleman--survived
political sabotage from then-mayor Frank Rizzo's
office. The effort suffered when improprieties in
the program's management discredited Coleman.
Nevertheless, the program had garnered sufficient
support to withstand the difficulties and become
fully operational again. Detroit's efforts have
not had the consistent support of any important
political figure. Participation in the program,
federally and locally enacted, has not been a
major administrative initiative.

3. The directives of federally legislated
programs are variably consonant with the
implementers' preferences. The national purpose
for urban homesteading was to relieve the federal
government's responsibility for a voluminous
inventory of vacant properties. The cities agreed
that urban homesteading could help alleviate
blight, but they differed with the legislation on
such matters as neighborhood and social targeting.
The local goals of Detroit and Philadelphia to
provide low- and moderate-income housing
opportunities were inconsistent with the quality
of homesteading properties and the resources
available. As a consequence, the Detroit program
made little progress and Philadelphia violated
program procedures to meet its goal. Baltimore's
local goal was not compatible with the Section 810
restriction of scattered site homesteading. As a
result, Baltimore made little use of the program.

4. The fiscal condition of a locality will
influence its proclivity to apply for federal
funds. Robert Stein found that there are
obstacles such as nontransferable costs that
impede grant seeking among some potential applicants. These expenditures (application, implementation, and opportunity costs) have the most
adverse effects on small communities.[16] The
history of federal involvement in all three
subject cities would suggest a corollary--previous
success in receiving federal grants may result in
their applying for programs ultimately unadaptable
to local conditions. The implementation planning
model recognizes that it may fail due to the
unfeasibility of the original plan.[17] In
evaluating unsuccessful efforts one must ask
whether the program was feasible and, if not, why
cities applied.

Political and fiscal circumstances will also
influence the likelihood of cities applying for
federal funds.   On the fiscal side, each city was
faced with some degree of   stress.   In such times
of   fiscal   austerity,   local   governments   might
better use   outside funds to   hold down   taxes and
maintain basic services.   Although participation
in urban homesteading was not mandatory, each city
would have   been   politically   hard-pressed   to
explain why it neglected to use the opportunity to
participate   in a   program with   the potential   of
Section 810 Urban Homesteading.   All three cities
had large   volumes of vacant   properties; Detroit
and   Philadelphia   had   particularly   high
concentrations of HUD-owned structures among them.
With the largest inventory   of vacant HUD housing,
Detroit   was   positioned   to   receive   the most
criticism.   By   the   time the   city submitted   an
application for   Section   810   Urban Homesteading,
the model had been glamorized in the media and its
"successes"   in   Baltimore,   Philadelphia,   and
elsewhere   were well   known.   Less   consideration
should be given to political pressures that result
in untenable situations,   as observed in Detroit's
operation.

5.   <u>Variable   mutual   adaptation   will   occur
between   the   federal   program   and   the   implementing
agency</u>.   Berman   found   that   mutual   adaptation
produces   the   most positive   program   outcomes.[18]
Urban   homesteading provided   the opportunity   for
each   city to   adapt   the   project plan   to   local
conditions   and   uniquely to   deliverer   behavior.
The deliverers   are the agencies empowered   to run
the   programs.   Baltimore,   in   minimizing   the
Section   810,   was   less   willing   to   make
organizational   accommodations   to   operate   and
retain   the program.   Nor   was there   sufficient
incentive to   make further   attempts to   adapt the
program   to organizational   behavior   with so   few
properties available.

Philadelphia   unsuccessfully   attempted   to
balance the   scale of adaptation   in favor   of the
organization.   Oversight by the   local HUD office
required   Philadelphia   to   adapt   to   program
stipulations or risk loss   of the program.   Local
officials   apparently   decided   that   the   program
benefits   were   too   great   to   lose   and/or   the
political   costs   were   too   high   to   bear.
Reluctantly,   a substantial   amount of   deliverer
adaptation   occurred   in   Philadelphia through   the
monitoring process.

Detroit   adapted   organizational   behavior   to
accommodate Section 810,   first   and foremost,   by
establishing and   staffing a line unit   to operate
the   program.   Despite   marginal   output,
modification of   local Section   810 goals   did not

occur. The actions of city officials, though, could be described as cautious in conforming to program conditions: (1) the city chose to set up its own as-is Urban Homesteading Program to pursue options not available under Section 810--namely, scattered site operation and independent arrangement of financing; (2) the city responded to complaints from housing activists--e.g., allegations by ACORN that Section 810 did not meet low-income needs--by blaming federal guidelines. It will be of interest in the future to see if Detroit officials respond to changes in the regulations that now promote low-income homesteading and the marked decrease in the city's Section 810 funding allocation.

6. The supply of federal incentives can influence local participation and program outcomes. Vacant houses were the incentive offered to participants by the federal government in Section 810. The scope of incentives was not enough to make a major impact nationwide or to induce greater cooperation by localities. Officials in each city studied felt that the assistance offered had serious limitations. Thomas Jaudon, a Baltimore DHCD official, remarked that Section 810 "offered just some houses."[19]

Without support for administration and rehabilitation in the Section 810 package, program implementers incurred the requisite additional costs. To fully accept this burden, a greater incentive is necessary. The limited supply of federal incentives was also a source of failure in the New Towns In-Town project.[20]

It is not clear how much additional support would be needed to exact greater commitment to urban homesteading, particularly where the concept is not suitable for local conditions or does not address local objectives.

URBAN HOMESTEADING: A UNIQUE FEDERAL PROGRAM

The following propositions about urban homesteading implementation reflect upon three unique program characteristics. Broader application of the underlying premises may be appropriate to other categorical programs.

Local feedback to federal legislators: The feedback to federal legislators from low-income housing advocates was an important force in the 1983 Section 810 legislative amendments. HUD put these amendments into effect with the regulatory changes promulgated in 1984. Similarly, in previous years, interest groups representing the poor were able to focus attention on CDBG program benefits for lower-income persons. These groups successfully managed the flow of information to HUD and Congress; therefore, they became powerful in setting agency agendas.[21]

Section 810 legislative changes occurred after a congressional hearing on urban homesteading, June 24, 1982. At that time, members and associates of ACORN from across the country criticized the program for its neglect of the low-income population. Subsequent legislation directly addressed their concerns by giving priority to lower-income persons, particularly those residing in substandard units and paying over 30 percent of their income for rent, and by extending time frames for rehabilitation and occupancy to promote sweat equity and discourage speculation. The regulations also narrowed the criteria for homesteader selection from those showing a "need for housing" and "the capacity to make repairs" to exclude those who owned other residential property (with a provision for hardship waivers). The two Urban Homesteading Demonstration Programs authorized by Congress in the Housing and Urban-Rural Recovery Act of 1983 had a low to moderate income focus. By using multi-family and locally owned properties, they could conceivably assist more lower-income groups by enlarging the inventory of eligible properties.

In a period of local autonomy and local public hearings for CDBG purposes, urban homesteading as a narrow-purpose categorical program provided a rare national forum to which low-income housing activists could appeal. The public policy arena comprises issue networks--webs of influence that operate at many levels of government with constantly changing participants. The low level of general interest in the program permitted activists a greater degree of influence than might be expected. Feedback on a program's performance is a powerful force in helping an agency fine-tune its administrative strategies. The loose-jointed play of influence provided opportunities to split and recombine the many sources of support and opposition that existed on policy issues.[22]

Dependence upon other federal programs: Section 810 Urban Homesteading relies upon CDBG for its survival. Nathan and Dommel described the CDBG program as a hybrid, in effect: an instrument of decentralization with many centralizing features.[23] Urban Homesteading has the opposite orientation: a centralization instrument with decentralizing features. Apparently, the elements favoring centralization and categorical programs have precluded the absorption of urban homesteading into the CDBG melting pot.

Financially and programmatically, urban homesteading has existed in the shadow of CDBG. The largesse of the CDBG Program, as the main source of community development revenue, naturally attracted more political and community interest at the federal and local levels. Section 810 legislation requiring target neighborhoods and comprehensive activities--while providing no administrative or rehabilitation funds--virtually locks the two programs together. CDBG regulations to increase the use of funds to principally benefit low- and moderate-income persons were introduced in 1978. Urban Homesteading regulations did not follow suit with low- moderate-income targeting until 1983, yet both programs had long been joined in attempting to meet the community development goals of their respective cities.

Its implicit link with the array of CDBG activities helps to explain why local implementation of the federal program can operate in so many different ways. On the one hand, urban homesteading could be viewed as symbiotic--operating toward mutual benefit within the CDBG fold. On the other hand, it could be seen as parasitic--a separate and distinct element of the community development effort usurping resources from other programs. Baltimore and Philadelphia programs fit the former model; Detroit the latter. Philadelphia has more fully integrated urban homesteading in its operation as related to low- moderate-income families. Urban homesteading director, Vincent Coles, commented in 1984 that homesteading would be likely to continue as an activity, even without federal assistance. Beyond that, he viewed most of Philadelphia's homeownership programs as variations on the urban homesteading theme.[24]

Baltimore definitely integrated the urban homesteading concept into its community development scheme--more noticeably in the case of its local initiative. DHCD disregarded HUD's insistence that local urban homesteading staff should be functionally distinguished from the other homeownership efforts. Paradoxically, While Section 810 legislation required program coordination, HUD area officials were moving toward functional fragmentation for monitoring purposes. In the meantime, urban homesteading as a local initiative proceeded--without federal intervention--toward meeting comprehensive goals in Baltimore.

Detroit includes urban homesteading among numerous housing programs to promote homeownership. Traditionally, home ownership for lower-income persons has been restricted. The stated urban homesteading goal represented an attempt to address the problem, albeit, inadequately. Adequate funds have not been redirected from the CDBG pot or other sources to run the federal or local programs effectively. Urban homesteading remains in competition with other programs for desperately needed resources.

Organizational capacity for implementation: Baltimore's reputation for strategic planning and its record of innovation and creativity with projects is formidable. Some housing policy analysts have determined that Baltimore has a superior organizational structure to carry out its housing- and community-development programs since all housing functions operate under an umbrella organization--DHCD. Recall that this plan emerged, in part, due to CDBG program consolidation. Although this structure works for Baltimore, it might not succeed in other cities. Downs has accurately noted that the larger an organization becomes, the poorer the coordination among its actions.[25] What may work in a smaller setting may not work as well in other, larger cities.

Philadelphia and Detroit also made organizational changes after the enactment of CDBG. Philadelphia established OHCD in 1976 and uses quasi-public agencies for a number of housing- and community-development programs. The city, as has been mentioned, maintains some control through the appointive process. This strategy can

circumvent the tedious city bureaucracy.   Obvious problems
are maintenance of authority and control, as evidenced in
PHCD's deviation from regulations.   Under Mayor Goode, the
city has set up an Office of Monitoring to address this
problem.
    Detroit's revised city charter,   adopted in 1974,
established the current community development agency.   While
not as encompassing as the Baltimore reorganization, some
splintered community development functions were combined.
Nonetheless, the most significant aspect of Detroit's urban
homesteading implementing agency is the functional
fragmentation.   As has been mentioned, a number of
functions--planning, building inspections, and zoning among
them--are shared with other departments.   Institutional
fragmentation complicates the achievement of organizational
objectives for recipients of federal aid.[26] Dispersion of
responsibility can make it difficult to obtain information
or to exert complete control over a program.   Detroit
experienced such a problem with regard to dual
rehabilitation inspections conducted by two departments.
    The extent to which urban homesteading and other
programs may be significantly affected by organizational
structure is a subject for future study.   All the cities
have made organizational adjustments to better accommodate
their principal funding source--CDBG.   Less extensive
modifications occurred to implement urban homesteading.   Yet
each city had a unique means of pursuing the disparate range
of CDBG and urban homesteading activities.   Further analysis
may disclose the suitability of various implementing
structures--specifically,   umbrella and nonprofit
organizations, or city line departments--for the attainment
of urban homesteading goals.   Each has its weaknesses and
strengths.

POLICY RECOMMENDATIONS

    Federal Section 810 Program

    Urban homesteading should be revamped to include all
elements necessary for full operation--rehabilitation and
administrative dollars as well as properties.   Without this
support, Section 810 implementation will continue to be
compromised.

    Local Policy Recommendations

    Baltimore.

The local program concluded as intended, and the federal
Urban Homesteading Program was closed out in December 1984.
The city does, however, operate other homeownership and

rehabilitation programs.   Although construction of new low-
and moderate-income   housing has been determined   more cost-
effective in Baltimore,   rehabilitation of existing housing
should be   offered as   an alternative.   Upper-income
homesteaders were subsidized to meet the local goal;   lower-
income residents should have an equal opportunity to upgrade
neighborhood housing conditions without   relocating to newly
developed sites.

Detroit.

Close-out of the Section 810 Program appears imminent.
Acquisition of eligible properties has come to a complete
halt.   Section 810 funding allocation was first severely
reduced and, later, eliminated. If the city cannot assemble
the requisite resources to finance loans to low-income
homesteaders and otherwise prepare them for home ownership,
the program should be revamped.   If the program is to
continue, it must do so with emphasis upon affordability for
potential homesteaders.   The housing needs of low- and
moderate-income people are complex and predicated upon their
limited resources.   The sizable low-income population in
Detroit might be better served by a line agency or division
with such a focus.   This notion is similar to the operation
of PHDC, but could function within the city bureaucracy. In
competition with the variety of housing, community,
commercial, and economic developments,   the interests of
lower-income persons are too easily shunted.

Philadelphia.

Steps should be taken to resolve the differences between
PHDC and   HUD before   they again   result in   program
interruption.   The success of the Section 810 Program there
depends upon the ability of local preferences and HUD
procedures to accommodate each other.   Recently invoked
changes may help in that regard.   By assuming monitoring
responsibility over PHDC,   the city administration is in a
position to mediate differences with HUD.   And PHDC, as
signatory to the Urban Homesteading Agreement, has been
thrust into a position of greater accountability.

General Policy Recommendations

Beyond the confines of this research, Section 810 Urban
Homesteading has provided an opportunity to consider (1) the
implementation of a   narrow-purpose categorical program
within an arena dominated by block grants and decentralization and (2) the improvement of federal-local government
interaction.
    Categorical program in decentralized arena: The caution
flag has already been raised about the likely adverse
impacts of block grant programs on benefits to lower-income
groups.   This study has shown that the possibility looms in

programs with local discretion over goals.   If at odds with
federal objectives, local preferences tend to prevail.
     Nathan and Dommel analyzed HUD jurisdictional disputes
based upon: (1) the type of issue involved and the grounds
for HUD's involvement;   (2) the importance of the issue to
both parties;   and (3) the outcome--whether HUD or the local
community prevailed.   Substantive issues ranked as most
important include strategy issues (involving the program mix
and the benefits by income group in the overall allocation
of   a   jurisdiction's CDBG grant)   and   program issues
(involving the definition and eligibility of specific
program   components of   a   jurisdiction's CDBG plan).
Procedural issues,   in order of importance, include
compliance,   involving such legal requirements as equal
opportunity,   environmental   protection,   Davis-Bacon
(prevailing wage), and citizen participation requirements.
Administrative and technical issues involve staffing, the
planning process, the rate of implementation, and the
various data required in CDBG plans and programs.
     The position of the local community tended to prevail on
substantive issues,   whereas HUD tended to prevail on
procedural issues.   Recipients are   more willing to
compromise on lower level particularly procedural issues but
are likely to resist HUD influence to defend their decision-
making prerogatives.[27] As urban homesteading is enacted in
other   areas,   the   factors that ultimately determine   "who
decides" and "who benefits" can be more fully explored.   A
mechanism to insure that program benefits reach their
intended clientele must be employed.

Federal-Local Interaction

     The interplay of control through regulations,   linked
funding sources (such as   Section 810,   Section 312,   and
CDBG),   and performance monitoring is likely to continue
across the breadth of federal programs.   Discretionary
monitoring of urban homesteading raises the basic question
of equity when disparate application is observed.   If
divergent goals are pursued by cities and field offices
monitor   the   programs   nonuniformly,   the   level   of
accountability to federal supporters will necessarily be
irregular.
     Well-directed monitoring at the field office level can
encourage consistency in monitoring objectives, strategies,
techniques, and local circumstances.   HUD and other federal
agencies involved in domestic affairs should promote regular
interaction with local program officials.   This could be
accomplished through intergovernmental committees and/or
task forces that collaborate on specific projects. Not only
might some of the ill-formed predispositions be dispelled
but ongoing, productive working relationships could develop
to the benefit of the program(s).   A federal official
explained how she learned about important city politics:
"It is basically filtering gossip and putting it
together . . ."[28] Through regular contact,   HUD staff could

become more attuned to what is happening--not only politically, but programmatically as well. More opportunities would exist for regular technical assistance in lieu of the yearly, but nebulous, threat of sanctions.

CONCLUSION

The history of federal programs and the actions of the three cities discussed suggest that urban homesteading, in some form, will continue. Philadelphia's intention to continue in this area was clearly expressed by a program official. Detroit's as-is program, developed subsequent to Section 810, will survive if homesteaders can secure financing. Cooperation of the private sector, which has not been forthcoming, is essential. Urban homesteading, as conceived to this point, has apparently run its course in Baltimore. That city's unprecedented use of UDAG funds to construct and rehabilitate housing for low- moderate-income households may further enhance its image as an innovator. All three cities are major laboratories for future exploration of federal program utilization.

Section 810 Urban Homesteading cannot be singularly charged with failing to improve low-income housing standards and upgrade neighborhoods. Its impact has always been limited by federal resource allocations, local conditions, and its own scope as a narrow-purpose program. The shortcomings of federal housing policy as a whole--many programs and projects--have left too many Americans seriously underhoused and the deterioration of once-vital neighborhoods unchecked. This study of Section 810 implementation has proposed some reasons for variations in program outcomes and some recommendations for improvement. Even at its best, Urban Homesteading can be expected to have only minor impact upon the complex housing problems of our society.

NOTES

1. The Washington Post, September 28, 1973, A-28.
2. Jeffrey L. Pressman and Aaron Wildavsky, Implementation (Berkeley and Los Angeles: University of California Press, 1973), p. xix.
3. Ibid., p. xxi.
4. HUD, Community Planning and Development, 1984 Consolidated Annual Report to Congress on Community Development Programs, p. 133.
5. HUD, Community Planning and Development, 1986 Consolidated Annual Report to Congress on Community Development Programs, p. 112.
6. Donald F. Kettl, The Regulation of American Federalism (Baton Rouge: Louisiana State University, 1983), p. 7.
7. Ibid., p. 43
8. HUD, "Urban Homesteading," Federal Register, p. 159.

9. Neal R. Pierce and Jay Hamilton, "'Flypaper Federalism'--States, Cities Want to Shed Rules That Accompany Aid," National Journal 13 (September 1981) 1636-39 (quoting ACIR Assistant Director, David B. Walker).

10. Terry Nichols Clark and Lorna Crowley Ferguson, City Money (New York: Columbia University Press) 1983, p. 231.

11. Concurrent with passage of the "Intergovernmental Review of Federal Programs," an Executive Order, HUD issued a notice (48 FR 29222, June 24, 1983) that deleted urban homesteading from the programs subject to intergovernmental review procedures.

12. Anthony Downs, Inside Bureaucracy (Boston: Little, Brown, 1967), p. 150.

13. Kettl, The Regulation of American Federalism, pp. 161-73.

14. Martha Derthick, New Towns In-Town, (Washington, D.C.: The Urban Institute, 1972), p. 83.

15. Ibid., p. 95.

16. Robert M. Stein, "The Allocation of Federal Aid Monies: The Synthesis of Demand-Side and Supply-Side Explanations," American Political Science Review 75 (June 1981), p. 335.

17. Pressman and Wildavsky, Implementation, p. 180.

18. Paul Berman, "The Study of Macro- and Micro-Implementation," Public Policy 26 (Spring 1978), p. 178.

19. Interview with Thomas Jaudon, Baltimore Department of Housing and Community Development, November 28, 1984.

20. Derthick, New Towns In-Town, p. 87.

21. Kettl, Regulation of American Federalism, p. 99.

22. Hugh Heclo, "Issue Networks and the Executive Establishment," in Anthony King, ed., The New American Political System (Washington, D.C.: American Enterprise Institute, 1978), p. 102.

23. Richard P. Nathan and Paul R. Dommel, "Federal-Local Relations Under Block Grants," Political Science Quarterly 93 (Fall 1978), p. 422.

24. Interview with Vincent Coles, Philadelphia Housing Development Corporation, November 15, 1984.

25. Downs, Inside Bureaucracy, p. 143.

26. Jeffrey L. Pressman, Federal Programs and City Politics, (Berkeley and Los Angeles: University of California Press, 1975), p. 112.

27. Nathan and Dommel, "Federal-Local Relations Under Block Grants," p. 430.

28. Pressman, Federal Programs, p. 87.

Bibliography

BOOKS

Abrams, Charles. Home Ownership for the Poor: A Program for Philadelphia. New York: Praeger Publications, 1970.

Anton, Thomas J. Federal Aid to Detroit. Washington, D.C.: The Brookings Institution, 1983.

Bardach, Eugene. The Implementation Game. Cambridge: MIT Press, 1977.

Barfield, Claude E. Rethinking Federalism. Washington, D.C.: American Enterprise Institute for Public Policy Research, 1981.

Brambilla, Roberto, and Gianni Longo. Learning from Baltimore. New York: Institute for Environmental Action, 1979.

Brown, Lawrence D., James W. Fossett, and Kenneth T. Palmer. The Changing Politics of Federal Grants. Washington, D.C.: The Brookings Institution, 1984.

Clark, Anne, and Zelma Rivin, Homesteading in Urban U.S.A. New York: Praeger Publications, 1977.

Clark, Terry Nichols, ed. Urban Policy Analysis, Vol. 21, Urban Affairs Annual Reviews, Beverly Hills, Calif.: Sage Publications, 1981.

Clark, Terry Nichols, and Lorna Crawley Ferguson. City Money, New York: Columbia University Press, 1983.

Crenson, Matthew A. Neighborhood Politics. Cambridge: Harvard University Press, 1983.

Dahl, Robert A. Who Governs? New Haven: Yale University Press, 1961.

David, Stephen M. and Paul E. Peterson, eds. Urban Politics and Public Policy. New York: Praeger Publishers, Inc., 1976.

Derthick, Martha. The Influence of Federal Grants. Cambridge: Harvard Univiversity Press, 1970.

Derthick, Martha. New Towns In-Town. Washington, D.C.: The Urban Institute, 1972.

Displacement: City Neighborhoods in Transition. Washington, D.C.: The National Urban Coalition, 1978.

Dommel, Paul R., J. S. Hall, V. E. Bach, L. Rubinowitz, L. L. Haley, J. S. Jackson, III. Decentralizing Urban Policy. Washington, D.C.: The Brookings Institution, 1982.

Downs, Anthony. Inside Bureaucracy. Boston: Little, Brown and Co., 1967.

Eisinger, Peter. The Politics of Displacement: Racial and Ethnic Transition in Three American Cities. New York: Academic Press, 1970.

Fish, Gertrude Sipperly, ed. The Story of Housing. New York: Macmillan Publishing, 1979.

Fossett, James W. Federal Aid to Big Cities: The Politics of Dependence. Washington, D.C.: The Brookings Institution, 1983.

Greenstone, J. David, and Paul E. Peterson. Race and Authority in Urban Politics. New York: Russell Sage Foundation, 1973.

Grigsby, William G., and Louis Rosenburg. Urban Housing Policy. New York: Center for Urban Policy Research, Rutgers University, 1979.

Grigsby, William G.; S. B. White, D. U. Levine, R. M. Kelly, M. R. Perelman, and G. L. and Clafen, Jr. Re-Thinking Housing and Community Development Policy. Philadelphia: University of Pennsylvania Press, 1977.

Guinther, John. Philadelphia: A Dream for the Keeping. Tulsa, Okla.: Continental Heritage Press, 1982.

Hale, George E. and Marian Leif Palley. The Politics of Federal Grants. Washington, D.C: Congressional Quarterly, 1981.

Henderson, J. Vernon, series ed., Robert D. Ebel, guest ed. Research in Urban Economics. Greenwich, Conn.: JAI Press, 1984.

Hughes, James W., and Kenneth D. Bleakly, Jr. Urban
Homesteading. New Brunswick, N.J.: The Center for Urban
Policy Research, Rutgers University, 1975.

International City Management Association. Municipal Year
Book. Washington, D. C.: International City Management
Association, 1962, 1972, 1983.

Jacobs, Barry G. Guide to Federal Housing Programs.
Washington, D.C.: The Bureau of National Affairs, 1982.

Jones, Bryan D. Governing Urban America. Boston: Little,
Brown, 1983.

Kettl, Donald F. The Regulation of American Federalism.
Baton Rouge: Louisiana State University Press, 1983.

Laska, Shirley Bradway, and Daphne Spain, eds. Back to the
City. New York: Permagon Press, 1980.

Levine, Charles L.; Irene S. Rubin, and George G.
Wolohojian. The Politics of Retrenchment, Beverly Hills,
Calif.: Sage Publications, 1981.

Listokin, David. The Dynamics of Housing Rehabilitation:
Macro- and Micro-Analyses. New Brunswick, N.J.: The Center
for Urban Policy Research, Rutgers University, 1983.

Macdonald, Michael C. D. America's Cities: A Report on the
Myth of Urban Renaissance. New York: Simon & Schuster,
1984.

McFarland, M. Carter. The Federal Government and Urban
Problems. Boulder, Colo.: Westview Press, 1978.

Muller, Peter O., et al. Metropolitan Philadelphia
Conflicts and Social Change. New York: Ballinger
Publishing, 1976.

Nathan, Richard P.; P. R. Dommel, S. F. Liebschutz, and M.
D. Morris. Block Grants for Community Development.
Washington, D.C.: The Brookings Institution. 1976.

Nenno, Mary K., and Paul C. Brophy. Housing and Local
Government. Washington, D.C.: International City
Management Association, 1982.

Palen, J. John and Bruce London, eds. Gentrification,
Displacement, and Neighborhood Revitalization. Albany,
N.Y.: SUNY Press, 1984.

Petshek, Kirk R. The Challenge of Urban Reform.
Philadelphia: Temple University Press, 1973.

Philadelphia Government, 7th ed. Philadelphia:
Philadelphia Economy League (Eastern Division), 1980.

Pressman, Jeffrey L. Federal Programs and City Politics.
Berkeley and Los Angeles: University of California Press,
1975.

Pressman, Jeffrey and Aaron Wildavsky. Implementation.
Berkeley and Los Angeles: University of California Press,
1973.

Rapkin, Chester and William Grigsby. Residential Renewal in
the Urban Core. Philadelphia: University of Pennsylvania
Press, 1960.

The Regional Science Institute. Functional and Economic
Interdependence in the Baltimore Region. Baltimore:
Regional Planning Council, 1970.

Rogers, David. The Management of Big Cities. Beverly
Hills, Calif.: Sage Publications, 1971.

Smith, Neil and Peter Williams, eds. Gentrification of the
City, Allen and Unwin, 1986.

Stegman, Michael A. Housing Investment in the Inner City:
The Dynamics of Decline. Cambridge: MIT Press, 1972.

Sternlieb, George. The Myth and Potential of Urban
Homesteading. New Brunswick, N.J.: Center for Urban Policy
Research, Rutgers University, 1974.

Sternlieb, George, and James Hughes. America's Housing:
Prospects and Problems. New Brunswick, N.J.: Center for
Urban Policy Research, Rutgers University, 1980.

Sundquist, James. Making Federalism Work. Washington,
D.C.: The Brookings Institution, 1969.

Urban Homesteading: Process and Potential. Washington,
D.C.: The National Urban Coalition, 1974.

Struyk, Raymond J., and David W. Rasmussen. A Housing
Strategy for the City of Detroit. Washington, D.C.: The
Urban Institute Press, 1981.

Weicher, John C. Housing: Federal Policies and Programs.
Washington, D.C.: American Enterprise Institute, 1980.

Wolman, Harold. Politics of Federal Housing. New York:
Dodd, 1971.

Wright, Deil S. Understanding Intergovernmental Relations.
Belmont, Calif.: Wadsworth Publishing Co., 1978.

ARTICLES

Abney, Glenn, and Thomas P. Lauth. "Influence of the Chief Executive on City Line Agencies," Public Administration Review 42 (March/April 1982):135-43.

Bachelor, Lynn, and Bryan D. Jones. "Managed Participation: Detroit's Neighborhood Opportunity Fund," Journal of Applied Behavioral Science 17 (October-November 1981):518-36.

Berman, Paul. "The Study of Macro- and Micro-Implementation," Public Policy 26 (Spring 1978):157-84.

Borgos, Seth. "The ACORN Squatters' Campaign," Social Policy (Summer 1984):17-26.

Browning, Rufus, Dale Marshall, and David Tabb. "Implementation and Social Change: Sources of Local Variation in Federal Social Programs," Policy Studies Journal 8, no. 4 (1980):616-32.

Bryant, Donald, Jr., and Henry W. McGee, Jr. "Gentrification and the Law: Combating Urban Displacement," Journal of Urban and Contemporary Law 25 (1983):43-144.

Clark, Anne, and Zelma Rivin. "Administrative Models of Urban Homesteading," Public Administration Review (May/June 1977):286-290.

Clark, Terry Nichols. "Local Fiscal Dynamics Under Old and New Federalisms," Urban Affairs Quarterly, 19, no. 1, (September 1983):55-74.

Cramer, Richard Ben. "Can the Best Mayor Win?" Esquire 102 (October 1984):57-72.

DeGiovanni, Frank F. "An Examination of Selection Consequences of Revitalization in Six U.S. Cities," Urban Studies 21 (August 1984): 245-59.

Dommel, Paul. "Housing Rehabilitation." In Housing Rehabilitation: Economic, Social and Policy Perspectives, pp. 68-72. Edited by David Listokin. New Brunswick, N.J.: Rutgers University Press, 1983.

Friedan, Bernard J., and Marshall Kaplan. "Urban Aid Comes Full Cycle," Civil Rights Digest 9 (Spring 1977):12-23.

Heclo, Hugh. "Issue Networks and the Executive Establishment." In The New American Political System, pp. 87-124. Edited by Anthony King. Washington, D.C.: American Enterprise Institute, 1978.

Heinberg, John D. "The Evolution of Rehabilitation as Public Policy." In Housing Rehabilitation: Economic, Social and Policy Perspectives, pp. 63-67. Edited by David Listokin. New Brunswick, N.J.: Rutgers University Press, 1983.

Henig, Jeffrey.   "Gentrification and Displacement Within Cities: A Comparative Analysis." Social Science Quarterly 61 (December 1980):638-52.

Lineberry, Robert L. and Edmund P. Fowler. "Reformism and Public Policies in American Cities." The American Political Science Review 61 (September 1971):701-16.

Lovell,   Catherine H.   "Coordinating   Federal Grants   from Below." Public Administration Review 39 (September/October 1979):432-39.

Lyons, William.   "Reform and Response in American Cities," Social Science Quarterly 59 (June 1978):118-31.

Morgan, David R., and John P. Pelissero, "Urban Policy: Does Political Structure Matter?" The American Political Science Review 74 (December 1980):999-1006.

Murphy,   Jerome T.   "Title I of ESEA: The Politics of Implementing Education Reform." Harvard Educational Review 41 (1971):35-63.

Nathan,   Richard P.   "State and Local Governments Under Federal Grants: Toward a Predictive Theory." Political Science Quarterly 98 (Spring 1983):47-57.

Nathan, Richard P., and Paul R. Dommel.   "Federal-Local Relations Under Block Grants." Political Science Quarterly 93 (Fall 1978):421-42.

Nelson, William E., Jr., and Winston Van Horne.   "Black Elected Administrators: The Trials of Office." Public Administration Review 34 (November/December 1974):526-33.

Pierce, Neal R., and Jay Hamilton. "'Flypaper Federalism'-- States, Cities Want to Shed Rules That Accompany Aid." National Journal 13 (September 1981):1636-39.

Rawson, George.   "Organizational Goals and Their Impact on the Policy Implementation Process." Policy Studies Journal 8 (1980):1109-18.

Sabatier, Paul, and Daniel Mazmanian.   "The Implementation of Public Policy: A Framework of Analysis," Symposium on Successful Policy Implementation. Policy Studies Journal 8 (1980):538-57.

Salisbury, Robert. "Urban Politics: The New Convergence of Power." The Journal of Politics 26 (1964):775-97.

Smith, Neil. "Toward a Theory of Gentrification." American Planning Association Journal 45 (October 1979):538-48.

Stein, Robert M. "The Allocation of Federal Aid Monies: The Synthesis of Demand-Side and Supply-Side Explanations." The American Political Science Review 75 (June 1981):334-43.

Sternlieb, George, R.W. Burchell, J.W. Hughes, and F.J. James. Housing Abandonment in the Urban Core." In Urban Politics and Public Policy: The City in Crisis, pp. 151-61. Edited by Stephen M. Davis and Paul E. Peterson. New York: Praeger, 1976.

Sumka, Howard J. "Implementing Federal Programs at the Local Level." Political Science Quarterly 94 (Fall 1979):419-34.

Thomas, Robert. "Implementing Federal Programs at the Local Level." Political Science Quarterly 94 (Fall 1979):419-34.

Van Allsburg, Mark. "Property Abandonment in Detroit." Wayne Law Review 20 (March 1974):845-88.

Weicher, John C. "Housing Block Grants for the United States." Urban Law and Policy 4 (1981):269-83.

Williamson, Richard S. "Block Grants: One Year Later." Journal of Legislation 10 (Summer 1983):277-95.

Wilson, James Q., and Edward C. Banfield. Public Regardingness as a Value Premise in Voting Behavior," American Political Science Review 58 (December 1964):876-87.

UNPUBLISHED WORKS

Cronin, Francis J. and David W. Rasmussen. "Tenure-Locational Choices in Detroit." Working paper 1375-3, Urban Institute, Washington, D.C., 1980.

Detroit. "Annual Overall Economic Development Progress Report and Program Projection." June 30, 1983.

Drew, Joseph. "Three Area Agencies: Government Contracting, Service Delivery and Bureaucratic Performance." Ph.D. diss., Detroit: Wayne State University, 1982.

Jones, Bryan D. "Decision at Milwaukee Junction: Community Leadership and Corporate Power." 1984 ms.

Mortimer, Henry L. "Philadelphia Case Study." Washington, D.C.: Urban Institute, 1978.

Schnare, Ann B.   "Household Mobility in Urban Homesteading
Neighborhoods: Implications   for   Displacement."   Urban
Systems Research and Engineering, Inc.   March 1979.

Sumka,   Howard.   "Urban   Homesteading."   HUD.   Washington,
D.C., 1981.

Office of Community Planning and Development.   "Fourth
Annual   Report   on   the   Urban   Homesteading   Program,"
Washington, D.C., n.d.

Varady, David P.   "Neighborhood Revitalization in the Inner
City: A Case Study of the Urban Homesteading Demonstration
Neighborhoods."   Paper presented at   the National Meeting of
the American Planning Association,   Seattle, Wash.,   April
18, 1983.

GOVERNMENT DOCUMENTS (by date)

1986 Consolidated Annual Report to Congress on Community
Development Programs.   Washington, D.C.:   GPO, 1986.

1985 Consolidated Annual Report to Congress on Community
Development Programs.   Washington, D.C.:   GPO, 1985.

"Announcement of the Local Property Urban Homesteading
Demonstration Program."   Federal Register 49 no.   184.
September 20, 1984.

Baltimore.   Community Development in Baltimore: March 1975
through December 1983.   1984.

1984 Consolidated Annual Report to Congress on Community
Development Programs.   Washington, D.C.:   GPO, 1984.

Annual Block Grant Monitoring Report,   City of Detroit: A
Review of 1981 Grant.   Washington, D.C.:   GPO, 1983.

Community Planning and Development Handbook.   Washington,
D.C.:   GPO, 1983.

Department of Commerce.   Bureau of the Census.   City
Government Finances 1982-1983.   Washington,   D.C.:   GPO,
1983.

1983 Consolidated Annual Report to Congress on Community
Development Programs.   Washington, D.C.:   GPO, 1983.

Congress.   House Subcommittee on Housing and Community
Development of the Committee on Banking, Finance and Urban
Affairs.   Urban Homesteading and HUD-Owned Abandoned Homes.
97th Congress, 2d sess. 1982.

Philadelphia.   Office of Housing and Community Development, Application for Federal Assistance. August 16, 1982.

The President's   National Urban Policy Report,   1982. Washington, D.C.: GPO, 1982.

1982 Consolidated Annual Report to Congress on Community Development Programs. Washington, D.C.: GPO, 1982.

Evaluation of the Urban Homesteading Demonstration Program: Final Report. 5 vols. Washington, D.C.: GPO, 1981.

Baltimore.   Section 810 Urban Homesteading Program Application for the Park Heights Community.   January 7, 1980.

Rules and Regulations, "Urban Homesteading." Federal Register Vol. 45, No. 7 August 1980.

Detroit. Application for the Urban Homesteading Program. June 19, 1979.

Evaluation of the Urban Homesteading Demonstration Program. Third Annual Report. Washington, D.C.: GPO, 1979.

Report to the Congress of the United States.   Urban Homesteading: A Good Program Needing Improvement. Washington, D.C.: GPO, 1979.

Community Development Block Grant Program: Fourth Annual Report. Washington, D.C.: GPO, 1978.

Evaluation of the Urban Homesteading Program. Second Annual Report. Washington, D.C.: GPO, 1978.

Proposed Rules, "Urban Homesteading Program." Federal Register 43, no. 105 May 31, 1978. 23692-9.

Report to the Congress of the United States. Housing Abandonment: A National Problem Needing New Solutions. Washington, D.C.: GPO, 1978.

The Urban Homesteading Catalog.   Washington, D.C.: GPO, 1977.   Baltimore. Department of Housing and Community Development, Homesteading--The Second Year, 1975. 1976.

Community Development Block Grant Program: First Annual Report. Washington, D.C.: GPO, 1974.

Congress. House Subcommittee of the Committee on Government
Operations. Defaults on FHA-Insured Mortgages (Part 2).
92nd Congress, 2d sess. 1972.

Comptroller General.   Report to the Congress,   March 19,
1971. Problems in the Program for Rehabilitating Housing to
Provide Homes for Low-Income Families in Philadelphia, PA.
HUD, B-118718. Washington, D.C.: GPO, 1971.

NEWSPAPERS

The Christian Science Monitor April 19, 1985.   The New York
Times, January 6, 1976-October 17, 1986.

The Washington Post, April 19, 1976-November 24, 1984.

INTERVIEWS

Andrews, Ellsworth. HUD. Baltimore Area Office.   November
28, 1984.

Coles,   Vincent.   Philadelphia   Housing   Development
Corporation. November 15, 1984.

Gee, Alan.   Baltimore Department of Housing and Community
Development. March 11, 1988.

Jaudon,   Thomas.   Baltimore Department of Housing and
Community Development. November 28, 1984.

Kiihr, Ken. Detroit Area Office.   June 20, 1985.

Kiihr, Ken. Detroit Area Office.   March 9, 1988.

Meyer, Pat, and Paul Dornan.   National Headquarters.
October 15, 1984.

Mhoon, Jo. Detroit Area Office. January 17, 1985.

Paul, Richard. Detroit Area Office. May 15, 1985.

Rhodeside, Stephen. HUD, Philadelphia Area Office. November
15, 1984.

Roanhouse,   Michael.   HUD,   National   Headquarters.
Washington, D.C. November 5, 1984.

Robinson, Julia. Philadelphia Office of Housing.   November
15, 1984.

Thomas, Albert.   Department of Building and Safety
Engineering, Detroit. Telephone interview. March 11, 1988.

White, Russell. Community and Economic Development Department. Detroit. January 23, 1985.

White, Russell. Community and Economic Development Department. Detroit. March 9, 1988.

Woodson, Kenneth. Philadelphia Housing Development Corporation. Telephone interview. March 2, 1988.

Index

About the Author

MITTIE OLION CHANDLER is a member of the Department of Urban Affairs at Cleveland State University.

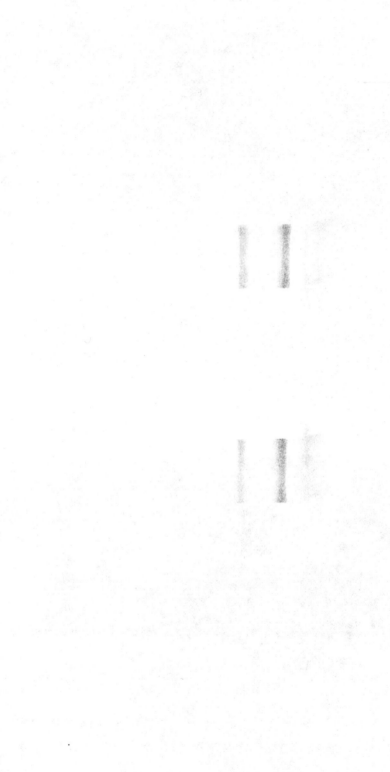